Helen Razer is a Melbourne resident. She is 31. She enjoys pay television, the Barkly Street Takeaway and avoiding society. She is a regular columnist for *The Age* and does the odd bit of telly. She is finishing her first novel called *Fat* for Random House which focuses on digestive urgency, real time obsolescence and infommercials.

Also by Helen Razer

Three Beers and a Chinese Meal, with Mikey Robins
In Pursuit of Hygiene
Everything's Fine

Gas Smells Awful
The Mechanics of Being a Nutcase
HELEN RAZER

RANDOM HOUSE AUSTRALIA

Random House Australia Pty Ltd
20 Alfred Street, Milsons Point, NSW 2061
http://www.randomhouse.com.au

Sydney   New York   Toronto
London   Auckland   Johannesburg

First published 1999

Copyright © Helen Razer 1999

All rights reserved. No part of this publication may be reproduced, stored in a retrieval system, or transmitted in any form or by any means, electronic, mechanical, photocopying, recording or otherwise, without the prior written permission of the Publisher.

National Library of Australia
Cataloguing-in-Publication Data

Razer, Helen.
  Gas smells awful : the mechanics of being a nutcase.

  ISBN 0 091 84002 3.
  1. Razer, Helen. 2. Depression, Mental – Popular works. 3. Anxiety – Popular works. 4. Self-help techniques. I. Title.

616.8527

Design by Yolande Gray
Typeset by Midland Typesetters, Maryborough, Victoria
Printed and bound by Griffin Press, Netley, South Australia

10 9 8 7 6 5 4 3 2 1

This book contains non-specific, general advice and should not be relied on as a substitute for personal counselling or medical consultation. The author and the publisher cannot accept responsibility for any consequence arising out of any negligent misstatement or other error contained within this book or any failure of a reader to obtain appropriate professional medical advice.

Acknowledgements

Helen wishes to give tongue baths to:
My family and ballast, Julie, Trevor, Meg and Darren. The prescient, fearless and chic Poppy King of Poppy Industries. The wilfully blonde and reluctantly clever Fiona Horne of manifold and excellent pursuits. The leftie stalwart and unusually ecstatic Eleanor Thornton who inheres in all things. The insurgent collaborator and deft telemanipulator Chris Gilbey of www.2000aware.com and other bits. The absurdly wholesome yet graciously sage Jen Oldershaw of ABC Radio. The happy purveyor of agitprop and sheer acuity, Helen Grasswill of 'Australian Story' on ABC TV. And Bruno too, of course, who makes great art and lavish dinners. The violently joyous and contentedly brilliant Dennis Watkins of many discerning projects. The proof that heterosexual monogamy CAN work, Lynne Haultaine and Frances Leach of ABC Radio and my idle youth. The robust Jonathan Green of *The Age*. My new co-conspirators at Artist Services, Maryanne Carroll, Elisa Tranter, Kylie 'Norgasbord' Connell and Sir Steve Vizard for affording me the most fraught eight weeks of my life. John Olb, you bloody rock, son. And so do you, Shauna Kane. The relentlessly adolescent and modish Jane Palfreyman of Random House. The frequently belligerent Susan King of Antediluvian Rocking Horse

and Naga Vigil and Psy Harmonics and things too numerous to mention. The folks of St Kilda for not sniffing indecorously at my Newtown residue. Also, my online partners in difference. Particularly liaminski and anyone else who made me read Fredric Jameson and Walter Benjamin. And, of course, Liquidscissors who gives the best text of them all. You know I dig you with all of my de-centred being and have not cybered anyone since we first collided and I wouldn't even THINK of bludgeoning myself with Situationism and bloody doof music for anyone other than you. Let's flesh meet. I think we'd get on. Also, the remarkable freelance hippie, Julia Stiles and Kim Swivel of Random House for knocking this amorphous beast into some kind of shape.

CONTENTS

INTRODUCTION
A RAMBLING RATIONALE
1

CHAPTER *One*
WHY AM I A FRUITLOOP AND DO I
ACTUALLY GIVE A SHIT?
11

CHAPTER *Two*
GET PAST THE ANGER, MAN;
YOU'VE EARNED THE RIGHT TO YOUR HISSY FIT
31

CHAPTER *Three*
WELL, MISS HIGH AND MIGHTY,
HOW DO I STOP CRYING ABOUT MY POTTY TRAINING
QUITE SO MUCH?
49

CHAPTER *Four*
WELL, MISS SELF-APPOINTED NOODLE CLINICIAN, I'M
SEEING A SHRINKY,
SO WHY AM I FEELING WORSE?
73

CHAPTER *Five*
NEURAL TRANSMISSIONS AND BAD BEHAVIOUR
97

CHAPTER *Six*
TECHNIQUES FOR SURVIVING DEPRESSION
109

CHAPTER *Seven*
LIVING WITH ANXIETY
127

CHAPTER *Eight*
FIRST AID
155

CHAPTER *Nine*
THE UNSPEAKABLE HORROR OF OTHER PEOPLE
177

CHAPTER *Ten*
NOW LISTEN HERE, SO-CALLED SUPPORT NETWORK
215

EPILOGUE
BECOMING A MUTABLE PROTAGONIST
223

WHO TO CONTACT IN AN EMERGENCY
227

BIBLIOGRAPHY
230

Introduction

A Rambling Rationale

IN WRITING THIS BOOK I have to admit to more than a little guilt and ambivalence. Then again, I have been owning up to guilt and ambivalence at just about every biweekly therapy session for the last couple of months now, so what's new?

Like any mildly deranged, hyper-rationalising human mess, I am compelled by a force more malevolent than even 'Australia's Funniest Home Video' to endlessly justify EVERYTHING I DO! So bear with me. I feel that I owe you an explanation. You did, after all, go to all the trouble of obtaining this specious tome, and you paid money you should probably have spent on Zoloft . . .

If, like me, you are a listless demi-fruitbat who is as disdainful of human society as you are indolent and depressed, then I am REALLY SORRY. Apologetic for the fact that you find it impossible, on occasion, to drag yourself out of bed; deeply humbled in the knowledge that you find your malaise ineffable, that your cosier relationships have turned to shit and that the only fibre in your neglectful diet comes in the form of a mistakenly swallowed fragment of an antidepressant pill packet.

It's sad and it's boring to be sick in the head, and until *Prozac*

Nation was published, it wasn't even faintly hip. Depression, anxiety disorder, dysthymia or whatever one chooses to call whatever the amorphous thing, or things, so many of us seem to wrestle with, is unglamorous CRAP. And I'm sorry. I'm not only sorry because, just like you, I have casually managed to acquire responsibility for every single misdeed enacted in the second common-era millennium, I'M JUST SORRY ABOUT EVERYTHING. (I'm considering, as it happens, the acquisition of an apologetic brand on my forehead. A tattoo that says, Sorry. I'm sorry. I'm just sorry for fucking everything.)

I'm also sorry because, in purchasing, shoplifting or borrowing this monograph, you may have been so addled that you actually thought it might help you get thoroughly well. It won't. At the incredible risk of sounding like a noisome hippy, Baby, the only person who is gonna make you better is you. I'm just some dickhead.

At the very most I can aspire to be Little Miss Parallax. I can perhaps afford some fleeting perspective (ugh, don't you abhor that word, aren't you sick of people telling you to get some?) and—a girl can only hope!—send you reeling haphazardly off in something approximating the right direction. The terrible news is: getting well is difficult, passivity is toxic, and overcoming THE THING is, more than likely, going to be the most troublesome encounter you've ever had. More irksome, even, than a new-age encounter weekend, a Kenny G live performance and a Tom Cruise film festival cubed. There isn't a single pamphlet, seminar or drug on earth that will completely deliver you from the melancholic mud. Getting better, or at the very least configuring some partial version of mental health that actually works for you, is a total shit fight.

Gas *Smells* Awful

So, there you are.

As a fellow neurotic, I profoundly appreciate the effort you have gone to in procuring this book. I acknowledge that the trajectory from bed to anywhere may be fraught with real danger. But PLEASE don't be pissed off with me if you have not transmutated into a Pollyanna On Steroids type by Chapter Three. You're a sick and overtly sensitive little puppy right now, and there is no way that the autotherapeutic blandishments of a thirty-year-old punk-rock ex-DJ are going to fix you up. What did you expect? I never claimed to be a conflation of Susan Powter and Carl Jung! Only the other afternoon I burst into inexplicable tears in the frozen dairy dessert aisle, had a nihilistic episode in tinned vegetables, and by the time I had oozed over to fresh produce had planned my tastefully ascetic funeral. I am no authority on emotional stability. I'm sick too.

I'm a mess. But perhaps I can assist a little. Because when I was REALLY sick, as opposed to the micro-manageable miseryguts I have become, I actually found it salutary to talk to people as fucked up as I was. Although I discovered great solace in grown-up and responsible psychotherapy, and despite the fact that I found the company of those who had 'healed' beyond suture inspiring, I craved the problematic companionship of those who were still substantially ragged. It is only those inhabiting the disparate realm of depression who legitimately understand that sparrows can be as huge and predatory as pterodactyls, that a particular street can be as genuinely terrifying as Sarajevo, and that a mildly mawkish advertisement for a phone company can be enough to double your dosage of Selective Serotonin Reuptake Inhibitors for a month. So if you wish fervently to interface with someone as crazy as yourself, then perhaps it is proper to continue reading . . .

Just in case you were wondering, your authoress *is* still a little fractured at the time of writing. Symbolic order still threatens to unfurl or melt in front of my very gaze. I carry a brown paper bag with me everywhere I go in case of hyperventilation, and at least once a week I'm pretty damn certain that I'm going to die. I'm still taking an antidepressive drug called Serzone; I always keep a Xanax handy and my shrink still gets to find new ways to answer my plea of 'I mean really, what's the fucking point and why in hell should I bother?' twice a week. I am certain he looks forward to my robust pronouncements. Not. Poor lamb. (You see. We are even capable of proffering profuse apology to our shrink! We are even capable of blurting abject contrition while simultaneously paying one hundred and seventy bucks an hour! I mean, TRULY, he could have procured an orthopaedic degree or some other career path that did not demand the manful endurance of one bitter girl's expert self-loathing.)

Doubtless some of you will now be remonstrating, 'Get over yourself, you self-indulgent milk cow. Ameliorate!' Others will coo, 'I've been there.' Still others will ruminate, 'Gee, what's SHE complaining about? Compared to me she's a psychoanalytic overachiever. I wonder if I send her a stamped self-addressed envelope, will she return it replete with spare happy pills?' All depressives and nervie pusscats find themselves at the nexus of such judgments, I have noticed. There are those who think you're plain lazy. There are those who lavishly and cloyingly feel your pain for you, and then there are those who just want to pinch your drugs.

No wonder you want to stay indoors with the blinds fastened and have quiet little panic attacks on your own! It's dangerous Out There.

In any case, I just wanted to let you know where I am. Just in case you're somewhere completely different. I can say, with absolute authenticity, I don't want to waste your time. Frankly, doll, I don't need the guilt. Got quite enough, thanks.

In getting this far, you have already expended precious energy. If you don't want to read a book by someone as nutty as yourself, by all means set it aside or demand a refund at once. Your efforts may be better expended on basket-weaving, negotiating the public transport network to your therapist, or just heaving your unwilling, untenably heavy and unwashed body out of bed.

Further, if you are one of those stalwarts who does not wish to subject her or himself to an egoistic account of another's relentlessly grey depression, scatter my text across the room. Do it now! Sadly, I am not a doctor. I'm just a chick in therapy who bears little or no authority and who must, therefore, write of her travails with the utmost (fractured) subjectivity. I can't offer anything more potent or wholesome than the techniques which finally pierced the unwholesome rind of my own depression and anxiety.

Finally, another warning. I have always believed that analogy can be devastating. I have always been suspicious of folk who nod effusively and impart 'I understand!' with dangerous zeal. I do not wish to impose sameness. I do not wish to deaden you by synthesising isomorphism. I don't know what it is like for you. So don't think I do. How could I? One can never truly exceed the boundaries of one's own experience. It is neither ethical nor possible. For example,

I would never presume to competently understand the lot of an indigenous Australian. How fucked must it be to see Wik overturned in Parliament? Sure, I bought the T-shirt and the armband, and if the Cipramil or whatever the hell I'm on has really kicked in by the year 2000, I'll be in the Compassionate Honky contingent just outside the Olympic stadium waving my Aboriginal flag. However, I'm not going to pretend that I know what it's like to be colonised, marginalised and whatever else. Plainly, we should value the particularity of each other's experience. Especially when it comes to going nutty.

I don't know which French philosopher wrote 'Metaphor is Death', but weren't they clever? The specificity of your own, her hum, mental disfurnishing can be submerged when you try to compare it to another. There is no way that your experience of, and eventual liberation from, despair is going to mirror mine. We are different, okay? And remember, your own depression and/or anxiety is special.

Our paths to and from utter, ostensibly hopeless confusion may be comparable at best. They will never be identical. In short, it is your nervous breakdown. You've earned it. Be proud of it. *Nobody* will ever be able to competently trace the complexity of your illness. Especially not me. I have sought sameness and contiguity, though. I have attempted to discern something that has a similar shape to my illness. I have looked for texts and filaments from popular culture that address me directly. I have attempted and presumed to mime the depressive illnesses of Dorothy Parker, Sylvia Plath, Kurt Cobain, Ian Curtis, Nick Cave, Patti Smith, Polly Jean Harvey, Mary Shelley, Gilles Deleuze and a galaxy of impressive others. Further, in the initial stages of my malady, I was simply desperate to 'identify' with anybody at all. Like a zealous convert to Alcoholics Anonymous, I projected the form of my sickness and continually saw it in others. In so vociferously 'identifying' with an assortment of deranged and talented, and not so deranged and talented people, I managed to quash my own 'identity'. The relationship you bear to yourself and your hissy fits is precious and particular. Don't supplant your problems with another's.

As much as I would like to chronicle in detail Your Own Personalised Torpor, I am incapable. On your own or with your therapist you must develop your own especial narrative. I could not devise and manage your story with any great resonance. You are the only possible architect of your own recovery. I KNOW that reads like dippy psylocibin-induced cop-out shite. I KNOW. And, incidentally, I'm sorry! (Just for a fucking change.) Know that I simply can't furnish you with the correct details. I can't provide you with an exact list of instructions. I cannot speak from any morass other than my own!

I do not wish to deny you your specificity. I do not wish, as so many do, to periodise our depression and anxiety and call it 'postmodernism' or 'slack' or 'blank irony' or something. You know, one could bang on about the torpor of the age. One could purloin Jean Baudrillard's schematisation of madness, for example, and write a shite book about how the hyper-real demands the presence of the neurotic. But Baudrillard does it so much better than I could. (You know, check him out if you feel like it. My favourite is *Simulacra and Simulation*.) And all I want to do here is write a little 'work'. A fairly closed, contained text that just helps a bit, you know? A small machine for you. I wish I were some fluid genius poststructuralist *über fraulein*. But I'm just some chick, yeah? Who is depressed and anxious. I can't offer any master discourse. I can't offer answers or final principles. What I can do, however, is provide you with some of the strategies and partial insights that have helped me manage. However resonant or however meaningless they may turn out to be.

Oh, and another thing. You will get better. You will get better. You will get better. Honestly. Even though you may suspect, as I often do, that anxiety and depression provide you with insights otherwise unavailable, contentment *is* do-able. Moreover, it is simultaneously possible NOT to hate yourself and the world and everything in it AND preserve your integrity. You're not buying any of this, are you? You damn depressed cynics!

In short, read this book only if you have the energy. Always embrace your own specificity. And remember, it does (eventually!) get better.

Sorry for all the exclamation marks. Sorry for the ostensibly Pollyanna-esque demeanour. Sorry for my lavish inability to proffer precise instructions. I'm just sorry. Okay?

Chapter *One*

Why am I a Fruitloop and do I Actually Give a Shit?

I HAVE WASTED MANY VALUABLE and expensive therapeutic hours searching for the origin of my distemper. Of course, I intend no disrespect to the psychotherapeutic tradition that demands a rigorous retelling of childhood trauma and all that. And NATURALLY there are some patients who find enormous relief in recovering threshold memories. The plain fact is some fruitloops, myself included, fairly much enjoyed a seamless, rosy infancy. Some of us cannot simply demand 'Why oh why?' and find an explanation or an origin for our dire, wan nuttiness. Sometimes there just isn't one. Our illness has no birth. Sometimes we bear no 'excuse'.

By contrast, some people have iron-clad reasons to be somewhat less than cheerful. The world is full of crap and some of you may have had to wrangle with some cumbersome problems. I do not suggest that you ignore these instances or marginalise or de-politicise them. Sexual and/or physical abuse is the most glaring case in point, of course. Involvement in a divorce or separation, grief and horrible relatives can all, similarly, send you around the twist. Further, losing a beloved pet can be traumatic. (I'm not taking the piss here. My beautiful Molly and Prudence spaniels passed on last year and I just did not cope.) Such incidents need to be remembered and properly addressed. Exploring your turbulent history is a matter for you and your shrink. I can't really help that much. But I can state that we human types appear to be able to resile, emotionally, from just about anything! A good shrink can help you find out exactly how elastic that poor damaged viscera of yours really is.

However, the act of unfastening one's own history should never be viewed as a cure in itself. The procedure of owning or reclaiming your past, however beneficial, is something to be completed and then put away.

Some people absolutely need to recover repressed memories. Some, like me, never shall. Because there are none to recover. Because the memories are too vast and chaotic. Because they inhere in the archaeology of knowledge as much as they do in the playground. Because all memories are adjacent to each other and written everywhere. Because your memories form part of one huge, palimpsest narrative for which there is no beginning or end. Because, to paraphrase Derrida badly, it is all just text. There is nothing outside or before the text. (Hey, I'm not being a total wanker. I will occasionally refer to texts which helped me. In the hope that they may help you also. May I recommend Jacques Derrida's *Writing and Difference*? It assisted me a lot.) Because we emerge into a nonstop dialogue and parts of us were invented long long ago. We will not trace the point of origin of the conversation or our 'neurotic' or 'depressed' involvement with it. Simply, there isn't a knowable, immutable beginning. To be a tosspot, we (nutty) subjects are always and already present in any interaction. All we can do is revise, refurbish and reassemble. There is no real value in remembering. And reconstruction is so much fun! No, really, it is.

Often we will never find a reason for our illness.

I have tried. And, actually, the worst thing that ever happened to baby Helen was that the other kids at school threw dictionaries at her head and called her a geek girl (before such a time as being a geek was cool or profitable). Still, I grew up to be a prize nutter.

I should accede here, dear subject, that I did have a putative 'reason' for my illness. Some bloke stalked me. Even though I did have a fairly tough time for about six months, getting death threats and unprovoked marriage proposals and upsetting visits at work from a person whom I didn't know and whacko letters about Bill Gates telecommuting into my mind, all of this crap really ceased to be the genesis of my complaint. Once I stopped so feverishly clutching at the 'truth' of being pursued by a nutter and (as far as I could perceive) relentlessly ignored by my diffident office management, it was just me and my illness. NATURALLY, in a situation like mine, you've got to protect yourself with restraining orders, bodyguards, rape alarms and knowledge of the Occupational Health and Safety Act and the like. This is just common sense. If you are in a dangerous or unhealthy situation, remove yourself from it. (And ladies or gents in putrescent and damaging relationships, I don't wanna hear any of that BUT HE/SHE LOVES ME shit. If he's/she's beating you up or fucking your best friend, patently he/she doesn't.)

When and if you do eventually relocate the supposed origin of your distress, it is of superordinate importance that you DO NOT fixate on this incident or series of events. Sure, you have to untangle it, pummel it about a bit and generally get mad with it. It is essential, however, not to allow it to inform your every word and gesture.

As Oprah would doubtless importune, it is good to be angry and, moreover, it is sensible to understand the shitty things that happen to you in a broad social context. Many bulimic acquaintances of mine, for example, have found that (a) an assiduous examination of their childhood history with food, and (b) the intercession of a body-positive feminism have helped mediate the tension between mouth and Ipecac or index finger. Understanding both a personal and sociological history can be wildly beneficial. Nobody here is arguing with that.

Enough with the whys and wherefores. On to:

BASIC GUILT MICRO-MANAGEMENT

I cannot count the conversations I have manfully endured with fellow depressives who squeal, 'But I'm not interesting enough to be insane!' Yes you bloody are.

Lots of us shaky people muddle about chastising ourselves for being sick. Frankly, this only serves to make us sicker still. There are so many other fabulous things to inspire your guilt on the road to getting tolerably well. The pharmacy bills you haven't paid, the people you weren't nice to, the sibling you screamed at, the shrink appointment you missed because you just couldn't prise your feculent, cumbersome self out of your odious bed for yet another day. Save your guilt and concern for where it is most urgently required.

You now know you don't need an elaborate justification for your illness, even though your alleged intimates will sometimes demand one. If your parents scream at you 'Where oh where did I go wrong?', just excuse their egotism and move on, problematic as it is.

(Unless they need to be told, of course. And even if they do need a good lecture, maybe it can wait. Maybe, on occasion, it can just go back to the fucking keeper. You know, I'm thoroughly full of shite. Unctuous hypocrite. Moi, I'm the least taciturn arsehole in the fucking universe! I love nothing better than to give people a verbose dose of what fucking for. I've just learnt, however, that often it is A WASTE OF MY TIME. And, in my own case, that it is better to screech for profit than for some intractable justice.)

If your partner or best friend takes your Funny Turns personally, you've got to just come over all Messianic and forgive them for mistakenly positing themselves at the centre of your universe. They know not what they do, et cetera and they are thick and stuff. There's an entire chapter devoted to coping with problematic and uncomprehending others later on, but a few words regarding their demands would be circumspect about now.

Remember when dealing with others: there are no reasons. So don't pay any heed to those who demand them. Believe me, I KNOW you're in no frame of mind to be a bountiful and benign perfect baby seraph and friend of the infant Jesus type right now. It's difficult not to reprimand ignorance in others, particularly if you happen to dig them rather a lot. But it is pretty easy to understand. When I think, in quieter moments, about my odd behaviour over the last little while, I have no great trouble perceiving it as fucking bizarre either. Why does Helen have to vomit when she enters the 2007 postcode? Why can't she remember her address? What the hell is going on with her handwriting? Why will she only eat white food this week? Is she ever going to get out of bed? Should we say something to her about the repugnant state of her plaid flannel nightgown? Does she realise she looks like a cross between some *Hound of the Baskervilles* nightmare extra and a Bay City Roller? And what is this thing she has about pineapple soap? Why does she spend so much time in the bathroom without getting clean? Why has she travelled down three dress sizes in as many weeks? What is the reason? Um, does that bitch ever actually sleep? Objectively speaking, these are not terribly unreasonable questions, but the folks around me have just had to accept (a) my weird turns and (b) the fact that I could offer no tenable explanation for them. (If it REALLY makes you feel better, I suppose you could tell people that you are allergic to some substance or other. And that it makes you do odd things. Maybe you could have a weird aversion to something like sweetcorn, car exhaust or something truly ubiquitous like carbon-based life forms. Invent an excuse for your strangeness if you must! Be creative.)

What seems like wilful swinish stupidity in others is merely the byproduct of our continued existence in a world where a linear understanding of EVERYTHING is endemic. People *will* demand that the narrative of your illness has a beginning, a climax and an end. And, the chances are high that you will also attempt to mimic the delineation of this structure. You will look for the start line. You will jog assiduously through your recovery. You will look to the end. My advice is bugger off this orthodox notion of progress. Don't look for beginnings, middles and ends. Just don't! YOU DON'T NEED A REASON. YOU DO NOT NEED TO LOCATE YOUR BEGINNING. THERE IS NO ACCEPTABLE 'PROGRESS'. THERE IS NO USUAL END-POINT. Some experiences of depression and anxiety may adhere to orthodox contours. Some, most, won't. 'Healing' (maan), or 'closure' (URGH), never arrives as an exotic, problem-free, neatly adorned little giftbox. (Wish it fucking did. Wish you could buy it at Coles.) Recovery does not follow a preordained trajectory. You may pronounce yourself thoroughly well and peaceful at 11 a.m. By three you could be comprised of brittle and nonsensical and brawling emotional filaments. You might very well be cowering under your doona once more, wailing, 'Why Oh Fucking Why?' to the cosmic grid. Neil Young is on the stereo again, you've decided that the cat is looking at you with furry pear-shaped intent and no-one but no-one fucking loves you. Or ever will. Oh, and you're fat. And that is the worst zit anyone has ever produced. People are laughing at you too. You are pathos personified. Et cetera. Yes, subjects, you may lose it completely just when you thought you were all neatly turned out and beautifully done. This will, inevitably, annoy you. And quite probably give other people the royal shits. Get ready for it. Warn others, if you must. Tell them that you are Unpredictable. But not in a cute and desirable personal-ad kind of way. More in the manner of liquid nitrogen.

Do try to believe me when I suggest that, at the very least, you are going to have to feign understanding of other people's confusion. Possibly you are going to have to simulate an understanding for yourself. Don't fret if the end to depression and anxiety is not yet in sight. Don't grumble if you cannot mine a reason for your sickening fear and panic. Don't give yourself a hard time if you weren't improperly potty trained as a youngster. You are just sick. And one day you will be well. It is unreasonable for you, or another, to savagely demand a reason. Bugger other people if they demand one. YOU DON'T NEED A REASON.

You may have ineffably long legs, natural blonde highlights, a charming liberal-minded family, peachy skin, a trust fund and an infancy that made the Waltons look tawdry and unwholesome by contrast. Well, certainly, I would have despised you at high school, and if I were the sort to attend therapy encounter seminars and I saw you across the room, you could be sure I'd be silently, persistently wishing for your death. But you can still have a thoroughly legitimate freakout if that is what your waspy heart desires. (Sorry. So much for my puissant victory over anger.)

If you do have complex reasons for your distemper, then unwind them. Search for that unclean kernel of 'truth'. When you've recovered it and confronted it in a thorough manner, taunt it, whack it, defecate on its repugnant visage and send it nasty letters.

Conversely, as mentioned, you may find that there is little or nothing to discover about your past. Further, you may find that you don't even discover any 'truths' about your 'foundation' or 'inner core'. If, like me, you engage for months and months in a strenuous unravelment and you find yourself merely comprised of dirty bandages with nothing at their centre, don't despair. There are so many other things that require your studious despair right now. The mere fact of finding an absence at your middle is irrelevant. (Actually, many able philosophers would argue that you have, in fact, arrived at a truth by distinguishing nothing. Many agile clever pants at the Sorbonne study for years to find out that they are empty. Feel special that you worked it out all on your own, okay? From Nietzsche to Blanchot, thinkers have questioned the Western assumption of a putamen—love that word, looks so sexy in print—or an inner self. Possibly, there is not one! There are a zillion books that address this notion. Email me or write if you need assistance in procuring titles.)

Pretty obviously I'm the kind of gal who loves a spot of critical theory, marginal gloss, analysis and subtext. However, at a certain point I had to put down the polymesmeric tome that was my life to date and just start thinking like a complete and utter junior dummy. Nuttiness is so toweringly involute that it can't simply be explained away. It cannot be explained or rendered 'correctly' at all. You can't reduce yourself. Nor gesture toward yourself and your condition with anything like accuracy. You are not a goddamn mathematical equation. Stop being a logician. Things might constantly unravel for a while and you simply cannot declare, If P Then Q. Some days, if P occurs, you might just handle it. On others, the appearance of the parlous P factor might mean you spend three hours weeping copiously, five hours contemplating suicide and ten hours with your dear sad nose cemented to a Homer Hudson hoboeken-crunch feed bag. You are not a knowable entity. You are not a predictable thing. You are, I suspect, more like a very difficult onion.

It is possible, from a purely philosophical standpoint, that we are all, in the manner of Streets' Viennetta dessert, simply Layer Upon Layer Upon Layer. (Is it just me and my deteriorating palate, or have those bastards started using nondairy ice confection and substandard compound chocolate?) The stuff of ourselves may not adhere to the classic epistemic model of an essence within a wrapping. Possibly, the essence, or history, we strive to discern so fitfully inheres in the wrapping. Perhaps, after all, we do not nurse stupendous immutable truths at our centre. Truths may be scored over us. There may be no difference between appearance and reality.

Perhaps your humblest most innocuous habits are as profound as your most cosseted and abstruse thoughts. Conceivably, the self is not a pure treat to be lovingly unwrapped. Maybe it is more evenly dispersed. Maybe I shouldn't be fucking with your poor already bruised head like this. But what did you expect from a tangled girl like me, dolphins and fucking wind-chimes? I already told you I was a nutter.

So what if you have no problematic history? Who cares? Concentrate on other things. Like the gardening and the regular self-administered Prozac perhaps. You do not have the time to worry about a hazy thing like an origin or a reason or a clue. You have way too many phobias and obsessive tendencies to indulge right at this interval. Don't worry about your past. Concentrate on your present distress. I, for example, must set aside a good fifteen minutes every day to worry about my eyes popping out of my head and my cortical fluid gushing out of my ears. Just a cute little quirk of mine. So the last thing I need to waste my delimited and sour energy on is guilt. I put an end to the anguish that arose upon discovering that I had no solid grounds for anxiety ages ago.

Don't worry about your emptiness. Don't be sad if there is nothing in your past and nothing at your core. If you find that you do not mime the traditional psychotherapeutic striptease, don't fucking worry. Personally, after months and months of assiduous therapy, I was shocked to learn exactly how facile I was. Some of us are all surface area. Some of us (especially the obscenely garrulous and self-regarding like me) have nothing much to talk about except pain. You may have nothing interesting in your gut. I didn't. Some of us have nothing to reveal. Some of us are not going to discover that we are both more complex and more beautiful than we initially suspected. I never found out anything that shocking or pleasant. My journey of self-discovery was actually pretty short. My internal landscape is kind of like Dubbo. Boring and Lenten and not terribly hard to navigate. This is not to imply, of course, that the therapeutic process cannot prove fascinating. You should just remember that you may not be fascinating! Well, obviously you are. But you might not recover a hidden truth. You may not mine a fabulous mystery. There May Be Nothing Of Value At Your Centre.

I am cognisant that I may be depressing you further. So, sorry. I just found this particular antifoundationalist perspective helpful, and it is my hope that you may also. In order to make this 'I am not complex not abstruse' sense of self work for you, obviously you're gonna have to readjust your value system. If you need proof of or legitimate ballast for this odd perspective, there is plenty. Lacan, Baudrillard, Deleuze, Irigaray, Cixous. For me, however, the route to reconciliation with my 'emptiness' was via Nietzsche. I read *Thus Spake Zarathustra* ages ago and pieces of it returned to me as I was refurbishing myself. (Friedrich would like the 'returning' I am sure.) Loads of people I know find esculent stuff in Nietzsche. Very hard to read without altering your assumptions about the construction of self. Further, even though this shuddering classic is over a century old, the contemporary reader will often discern a sense of familiarity within it. (Things seem to have a habit of disseminating, don't you find? Even if you haven't read Freud or heard Led Zeppelin or watched 'Sale Of The Fucking Century', you sort of know what they're about. Things reach you through the atmosphere. Specially old books with big names. They are a bit like nuclear power stations. We don't want to be near them; we know we should be frightened of them, but the radioactivity gets to us anyway. So what the fuck? Read difficult dangerous books. Risk radiation poisoning.)

Don't let the fact that you are completely vacuous AND insane give you the shits as well as everything else! No, just gagging. Of course you're not vacuous. You are, after all, quite fascinating enough to go loopy. But PLEASE don't worry if you DON'T come over all Visionary From Hell like and see the fucking albatross with black lips baked and throats unslaked and all of that shite. You know, if I have to compare my inner workings to a poetic verse, I'd probably proffer the 'Pat-a-cake Pat-a-cake' rather than 'Rime of the Ancient Fucking Mariner'. I am trying to say that a lot of us, particularly the ostensibly complex 'overthinker' types, already possess reasonable and intimate dollops of self-knowledge. You may have been profoundly analytical all your life. You can be crazy AND incorrigibly self-reflective. ALL AT ONCE. It's highly likely in fact. Clever nutters, despite their desire, are often disappointed that therapy offers them few revelations. You can be sick AND intimate with yourself. For example, I know quite a number of toweringly intelligent feminists, aware of the phallic ideal etc, who somehow manage to sustain terrible eating disorders. Why did they maintain their self-destruction when they knew the origin of it precisely? You know, they can read Faloudi or whoever until they are so sick that they don't even need to stick their fingers down their throat any more. But they still stick their fingers down their throats. Go figure. Really, it's possible to have an incendiary understanding of identity, structure and the order, or disorder, of things and still be a NUT.

Gas *Smells* Awful

Gilles Deleuze killed himself with smack a couple of years ago, and he's like the cleverest person who ever lived and completely re-signed psychoanalysis and stuff. He wrote a book with Guattari called *One Thousand Plateaus* about how contemporary structure *demands* insanity, for shit's sake. He knew mental illness, but still fell 'victim' to it. Intelligence or a passion for cultural studies is no prophylactic against depression. And, duh, really Helen, an interest in the order of all things appears, at times, to be almost a prerequisite for nuttiness. Or the other way around. Or something. OH I JUST DON'T KNOW ANY MORE. (Poor Gilles Deleuze. Upon learning of his death, I was very depressed, just for something fucking novel. But I did think, 'At least I might be able to finish all of his books one day, seeing as how he won't be writing any more.' Then I discovered Fredric Jameson, thanks to some online cleverclogs. And he's still alive and well, damnit.)

Just chill re the I Have No Reason business. There are, to my knowledge, no commonwealth bylaws that require written justification in triplicate for having a panic attack on the train to work. So what if your life has been a creamy pony dream up until now? Doesn't matter. Desist in saying, 'But as I am so jolly clever and involute and generally rather, her hum, brilliant even if I do say so myself, you'd rather think there'd be some pretty fucking fascinating detritus to look at inside of me.' Well there bloody well might not be anything much in there, okay? Just broken bits of pottery and old Christmas wrapping and the odd cheese sandwich. You've seen it all before.

One very basic thing my therapist said to me assisted me in overcoming my middle-ish-class guilt. The poor man was probably thoroughly bored with me demanding WHY OH WHY was I such a screw-up when my Dad always showed up on Father's Day at Brownies, my parents never divorced and no-one in my family called me a fuckwit when I wore a duffel coat, horn-rimmed spectacles and a false beard for two weeks straight insisting that I was an esteemed medieval historian? (Perhaps they should have. Poor little simulation of a man that I was.) My shrink just said, 'Look, Helen, panic attacks and depressive episodes are traumatic enough *in themselves* . . .' Bang. He was quite correct.

I felt, quite physically, illuminated at this juncture. Suddenly I didn't need some dark thing at my centre or in my past to help me get better. Hmmm. Let me explain this. I had imagined my illness and subsequent symptoms to be analogous with ripples in a pond. I thought that a particularly large pebble (significant motivating force for anxiety and depression) had been thrown into a large and deep body of water (why, the stultifying and stagnant pool of my illness in which I was immersed and in which I consisted, of course!). The boulder, naturally, represented my reason for being ill. I imagined the concentric circles radiating from the impact of this now deeply embedded rock. I assumed that the wake would eventually still and, when I had become aquatic and proficient and brave enough, I would dive to the bottom of the pond and retrieve the sedimentary miscreant! No such luck. I did not grow gills. In time I realised that I was not, and never had been, a Still Waters Run Deep kind of human. I was, I acknowledged, flailing about in a mere and evanescent puddle. One of those fuzzy subjects who drown in a perilous teacup of tepid liquid. Not even deep enough to secrete a stone. My illness was, I conceded, transparent and shallow. Helen is shallow, I realised one day. This, kids, is not what the self-help orthodoxy would call negative self-talk. It is a simple fact. I am capricious. I am not deep. I am, as far as the construction of my malady goes, pretty fucking fluid and ephemeral. Moreover, I am not residing in a discrete and serene body of water. I am a mere droplet. Fused to the earth, susceptible to the wind and in frequent contact with fire. Elemental blah. I am all these things. Everything impinges upon me and troubles me because, after all, I inhere in everything. And everything inheres in me. It is not bad to be shallow. And, upon this last point, Nietzsche is in firm accord with your troubled authoress.

When I fleshed out this 'shallow' metaphor, the ripples kind of stopped. When I acknowledged my susceptibility and my caprice, I calmed down. I finally steadied to a significant degree when I became less conceptually steady and separate. I did away with my history and looked the manifold currents of the world and myself square in the face. I learned to say, This Is Bad, But It Will Pass, with some conviction. My shape will change by this afternoon or tomorrow. Fuck history. Re-enter the world. Affirm your insouciant, impressionable dropletness, Helen. Embrace your mutability. Refuse your fallacious rigidity. And blah, blah, blah.

(I think the neighbours might have heard me enact this bizarre quasi-affirmation thrice daily. Oh well. They've endured my personally scripted love songs to their long-haired tabby cat as well. Further, they've spied my Friday evening black-candle rituals, generally involving a tattered photo of the ex, copious iron filings and very very loud DJ Spooky banging on about sophistry and such on the Sanyo. So evidence of a warped and resonant meditation was really the least of my worries, I suppose.)

Once I had accepted the trauma of mere existence, I really felt so much better. Once I learnt that a consummate and fixed comprehension of myself was (a) impossible (b) undesirable and (c) downright unhealthy, I began to get better. In short, when the entire concept of health became less fraught and demanding and more genuinely elastic, it did seem more attainable. I made the entire concept of sanity fit me. I turned it into a sort of One Size Fits All garment. Rather than a binding and abhorrently expensive size six Prada original. (Will my analogies EVER improve?) I just turned sanity into something wearable. I did not lower my expectations. I just had a pretty massive epistemic about-turn and confronted some shit about the construction of the self. (Oh, and I stopped popping benzos, too. That helped. Benzos may occasionally be useful. But I think they constitute some serious and addictive and stultifying shit, baby. Pills are fucked. But more of that later.)

Life alone, in my humble and unscholarly opinion, is sufficient reason for a crack up. And don't be guilty about the glaring non-presence of a conspicuous cause.

And one last word of warning: DON'T EVER trivialise your illness. Steadfastly refuse those slickly practical types who brandish obsolete phraseology like 'Generation X' and write dumb articles about how self-indulgent we are.

Folks can be so cruel and dismissive of depression and anxiety. They can all go straight to hell.

There is, currently, a lot of critique and needless humour about the dysthymic epidemic. You just have to sail quietly away from it. It is everywhere, seemingly, these days. For example, I remember getting royally pissed off when, upon reading yet another glib article seeking to misappropriate the suicide of Kurt Cobain for the imperious and smug weekend broadsheet Op Ed page, I was confronted with the conceited interrogation: isn't it appropriate that Generation X's appointed spokesperson died complaining of a tummy ache? (If you are a Kurt fan, as I am—and let's confront the awful truth, which depressive under the age of thirty-five is not?—you may recall that his suicide note gestured toward the fact of his persistent and virulent irritable bowel syndrome as a primary reason for his decision to die.) What the fuck is that supposed to prove, oh slick boomer nincompoop? Sure he wrote some plainly depressed stuff about his stomach hurting in a sad note that, after all, was none of our business. Well, my stomach has hurt a lot over the last little while. My shrink tells me that it is a fairly common symptom of depression. And some days, a painful stomach was just about enough to turn me into a crap Sunday tabloid article too. And sometimes it was a forgotten phone number or a runaway bus or the terrible realisation that I had run out of Poppy's excellent Inspiration lipstick with an all new moisturising unguent. It doesn't take much, some days. You know that. Depression and anxiety are some serious shit. Refuse to acknowledge or listen to the dunderheads who would have you believe otherwise.

The difference between Kurt and me of course (well, quite apart from the fact that I have not and will never achieve international status as an honoured iconoclast and all I can play on the guitar is a very poor medley version of 'Jane Says', 'Gloria' and 'Jail Break') is that I didn't actually get around to topping myself. Plainly, you haven't either. Gee, I've thought about it a lot, though. And so have you, more than likely. And, to be honest, I think that I may have actually tried it once. Well, I did. However, while I'm not yet at the point where I could wear a Choose Life sweatshirt, and I certainly don't amble about lightly praising all of nature's bounty, I'm quite relieved that my ambivalence, or multivalence, stopped me from killing myself. It is not that the world is ineffably brilliant. Most of it is utter shit. I just think we owe it to ourselves to get better. And there are flopsymopsy beagles and great bands and excellent and occasionally affordable facial treatments and chocolate croissants and novels by Martin Amis and one or two terribly worthwhile people to grumble with. Just as some tiny inconveniences can seem too much, some of the small and decent things can offer pretty substantial, if evanescent, globules of joy. Don't pretend you don't agree with me, grumpy. Are we ready to get better, oh querulous people? Come on, then.

Chapter Two

Get Past the Anger, Man; You've Earned the Right to your Hissy Fit

FINDING A CONTEXT FOR YOUR problems is fab. Confronting your past may prove essential. Personally, however, I genuinely believe that I wasted a lot of time being cross. On finding a reason and a history to be cross with. I spent trifling days and weeks and months blaming folks or social mores for my illness. I filled in my sour hours by inventing a whole host of new and fascinating germs for the full and overabundant flowering of my distress.

Of course, some of you won't be quite as adept at rage as I (gosh, I'm good at it), and such an anger deficiency probably translates to at least three months of total shrink-immersion. So go get really steamed up ASAP. When you get past the grief and the stasis and the obsessive Coco Pops consumption and whatever, though, anger can prove a formidable obstruction. Sometimes you can become immersed in it and end up choking on your own messy history. You have to let it go.

Allow your pure hate and omnipresent suspicion of injustice to go out on a wander. Let it go. It's gone. It's gone. It's gone. I have to repeat that to myself daily like some hippy dotard with a lung full of

Buddha heads, a barely roadworthy Kombi featuring free intuitive paint job and an Emerging Poet grant from the Australia Council. Oh, who cares, it helps. It's gone. It's gone. It's gone. If you are a cranky pants like Helen, you may wish to try it. Just make sure the shutters are ably fastened and no-one else is in the house. Even us nut-bars have an image to uphold.

I can sense the cynical reverberations at this juncture. Yet another pastel neurotic, I can hear you lament, banging on all missionary-like about forgiveness. Get past the anger, man. Wade through the blame. Well, forlorn as it may sound, I do think it is a good idea. (I would like to indicate, at this thorny point, that none of this bland acceptance-type cajolery I'm currently egesting should prevent you from becoming an activist, for example, when you are better. And I say this because a load of depressives I know tend toward Weltschmerz. The depressive seems disposed to acknowledging the presence of evil macro-systems etc and to being a bit of a do-gooder in general. So turning into a Big Bad Feminist, a Land Rights Activist or, hell, even a counsellor, are all healthy *eventual* responses to neurotic crap. Please do wait until you've stopped having panic attacks and suicidal afternoons, though. Nothing compromises a good cause more than nutcases like us falling hysterically to the floor while free-basing Valium and crying about how Daddy didn't love us enough and/or ever buy us a pony. Accept that you are not much use to anyone but yourself for a while.)

In recovery from anxiety and depression there comes an interstice where you just have to let the past drift off and disassemble on its own. Having imparted such wisdom-lite, however, I should probably concede that there are a couple of thousand people I would still dearly love to fucking king-hit. I have my shit list. Of course I do. You would absolutely HURL if you knew how much money I have spent on lawyers! I wanted to punish anybody who said anything negative about me. I wanted compensation monies. I wanted to sue for any and all of the fictitious infractions I could remember from 'LA Law'. Fortunately I found a lawyer who told me that I might be better off in a psychiatrist's office than in hers. At the risk of sounding like a faulty, hyperaware neomystic dolphin CD that keeps wanly hammering the same old fluffy homily home, LET IT GO.

It is easy to blame. It is so easy to become a necrophile. To maintain a freezing, sexy privity with the past. An online friend of mine says this constant *Being* in the past is sort of like masturbating to pornography. Tempting. Freezing. Kind of disgusting. Discourse and imaginary intercourse with an image of the self as an other. He recommends *Becoming* as a mode of life. (Gilles Deleuze makes the distinction between Being and Becoming in *The Logic of Sense*. Possibly the greatest book or machine ever anywhere. It is about the Alice books and identity. Being, briefly, is a type of a lie one tells oneself. That one is unified. That one can be all-knowing about the past and the future. Becoming is about 'being' multiply or infinitely divided—and perhaps happy—as one who exists from several different modes.) So, Becoming is recommended. Free yourself from the temptation of the past as much as you can.

Despite this patently vapid bent of forgiveness, you may be assured that I am LYING. We all know it is healthy, robust and sound to forgive. But I have not yet forgiven. I still blame history or others for my illness. In hating my history and my others, however, I reinvent them. I confer power upon them. I continue to allow them their primacy. I suppose that I am suggesting that you (and I) become unstuck. That we seek a new comprehension of time. That we forge a new way to posit ourselves in relation to the past and to others.

Of course, this is all a massive po-mo wank. And it is, of course, very difficult to learn how to Become. To learn how to exist in an entirely different mode. So some tactics are required in the meantime. (I am, at my putamen, a pragmatist after all. You know, you can only take Baudrillard, Virilio and all their friends so far in the desert of the real. Then you've just got to get well.)

HATING PEOPLE QUIETLY

The postidentity revolution hasn't happened yet. So sometimes one needs a little devilish ritual to help those evil others to be shriven. Propitiously, one of my dear friends is a witch and has instructed me in the ways of banishing and binding spells and suchlike. Actually, her name is Fiona Horne and she has written a very nice book of spells, illuminations and reflections called *Witch*, and within it my venerable panspiritual priestess advises a series of karma-free Wiccan solutions to the thorny problem of other people. (No hexing, mind. Which sort of pisses me off. Cos I'd love to give a few people genital warts or similar, you know? Apparently you have to be a way competent sorceress before you can consider that type of incendiary gear.) As a fairly immutable pragmatist myself, I don't really believe in that witchcraft palaver. But, as the eldritch architect of *Witch* will herself acknowledge, the spells may not be infallible, but gee they can make you feel better. Enacting magic can, genuinely, be calming. I recommend it. (There is, of course, much

Gas *Smells* Awful

Wiccan matter on the web. Spooky types and practices are generally quite easy to discern. They advertise freely these days.)

My mother (and sister in neurosis) and I have further followed Miss Fifi's advice and now regularly consult the tarot deck. Especially when one of us is having a funny turn. We prefer the multivalent power of the Waite cards, naturally, with their abundance of feminine specific symbolism. Whenever our nemesis gets the ten of swords as his or her last determining card, we rejoice! Well, it works for us. And it softens us and precludes the possibility of violence. Rather than hit someone with an obscene early morning phone call, I go to the Waite deck.

Further, a dear fluffy friend and occasional mentor—propriety prevents me from openly crediting the authoress of this cunning scheme—has developed an eerily brilliant figurative solution to hatred. When she has amassed untold fortune, as she shortly shall, she is going to email the Queen's jeweller with a request. A certain number of twenty four carat gold dildos, please sire, with the legend 'Go Fuck Yourself' stamped upon them in flawless white De Beers diamonds. Is this girl the conceptual granddaughter of Andy Warhol or what? I was very impressed, needless to impart, and have already offered Miss Thing a substantial cash donation. Disdain is always much better expressed with panache.

Then there is my friend Liquidscissors who just has a bath when she feels a fit of hatred coming on. She's very clean, and lavender scented most of the time of course.

Another risible revenge was recently suggested to me. This technique, intrinsically suburban and wholly masculine, involves the use of one's own penis. Overtly, a solely male vengeful pursuit. Which should only be earnestly attempted upon another male. As indicated by myself in other texts, the penis, with its proximity to the threshold signifier (that is the phallus, for people who haven't had the time to bother with neo-Freudianism) is always a fun instrument to employ. Gents, this exercise requires a spot of diligent planning. First, assume the demeanour of one with an injured shoulder for several weeks previous to a social gathering at which your enemy will appear. When an acceptable level of collective drunkenness is accrued at the event and you have thoroughly established the fact of your injury, approach your enemy with your visage arranged pathetically. Implore thus: 'Mate, my shoulder's buggered and I really need a piss. Do you reckon you could help me with the old fella?' According to certain witty exemplars of this awe-inspiring scheme, the man approached will generally accede to your demands. Although he may refuse to point your organ as you urinate, he will most certainly remove it from your trousers. This little ploy is deliciously deceptive, dirty and wrong in at least fifteen different ways. Its use should be reserved only for the most fulsomely repugnant.

Actually, don't do that. I just wove it into the text because I found it quite funny. So that's enough of that.

There are a host of other relatively harmless yet pleasingly nasty modes of ritual revenge. One of the most reliable and honourable, however, is to just wait for idiots to fuck up on their own. To let the past drown in its own bane. And, frankly, to give the arseholes enough rope. Naturally, karma is a load of shite and the world and all the things in it are NOT governed by an inalienable fundamental justice. However, trite as it is, those who contributed to your misery and distress are probably feeling even more rotten than you. Remember that. Don't feed on it too voraciously. Just cling to it briefly when you need to.

In short, being vengeful might be fun in the short-term, but it is a waste of fucking time. If I went about exacting revenge on all the bods and institutions whom I felt so richly deserved it, I'd never have time for therapy, fabulous vulpine dogs, substandard games of golf, dry vodka martinis, facials or any of the other things that actually keep me breathing. However, I can't really suggest with impunity Let Go Of The Past as I am so scored over with traces of it myself. But, you know, give it a good old Aussie go, I suppose. It is really rather key for you to assuage the venom. If you don't, you generally end up just wasting your time or, worse, fucking yourself up even harder. If you are Turning Your Anger Inward (urgh!!!) and fucking yourself up with maximum proficiency, go straight to the Bad Behaviour section in Chapter Five. (That one is especially for all you anorexics, drug-addled fiends, drunks, self-flagellators, promiscuous yet condom- unencumbered tarts of either gender, gamblers et cetera).

Problematic as it is, try to stop hating people in the initial stages of your recovery. Looking for a reason or an excuse can prove to be naught but a massive waste of time. And for now, let me assure you, nothing is more irritating to a fuckwit than your ability to outrun their fuckwittedness. The people who give you a hard time are going to HATE it when you stop blaming them. Impassivity, in a sense, can prove the best revenge. Or something. At the very least, try not to hang around with arseholes. And if you have to, please try to hover above them. Even, and most especially, if you are related to them. Even if you're sharing a bed and a life with an irksome weasel. We'll get to that later. We need an entire weighty chapter on dealing with those intimate turds! But for now, strive to believe me as I implore with deepest suburban intent, the best revenge is autonomous consummate insensibility and success. (Recovery is success.) These complementary twins have a knack of really getting up people you despise.

Stop pouting about the past. Stop pouting about not having anything to pout about. When you work out or, rather, *decide* that your pouting is not 'justified', that's generally when you start suffering from abject guilt. And guilt is shite. As previously inferred, I personally haven't got that much, on a global scale, to pout about. Pout vociferously, however, I do. And quake and hyperventilate and weep and cower and vomit. Dread, depression, dysthymia, dysfunction and the whole alliterative nine yards! For some time, after I had finished blaming ex-friends, stalkers, education policy-makers, the government, the patriarchy, 'Australia's Funniest Home Video' and my fifth grade Roman Catholic Scripture teacher's passional retelling of the Virgin Birth for everything, I began questioning my entitlement to illness. This is really stupid if you think about it. A lot of folk sashay about—well, they tend to skulk disconsolately rather than sashay buoyantly, as it happens—insisting I Have Not Earned This. As though depression and anxiety constitute some kind of prize! As though mental illness is a badge of honour only to be worn by the most battle-weary. As though hissy-fitdom is really a province to be inhabited by the most manfully besieged and frazzled.

As though it is some kind of fucking privilege. It's really dumb to think this way. Very widespread, however. Perhaps you think I'm an idiot. (Upon the odd occasion, I most decidedly am.) A sage friend of mine told me in the initial stage of my illness not to worry about 'why' and I called her an idiot. I thought this was an essential interrogatory. It's not. It's a crap and disingenuous and facile and fruitless way to spend an afternoon. Doesn't help you feel better. Excise 'why' from your lexicon for a day or so.

AFFIRMING AND APPROPRIATING

Attempt, please, to intone, 'I've Earned The Right To My Hissy Fit'. Yes, the brittle pragmatist is suggesting that you AFFIRM. ARGH. You know, this shit can work. It can help you 'change the program'. I mean, it's as embarrassing as all get out. But it does help. It is, of course, necessary to inject humour and something of yourself into the absurd and profoundly unhip process of affirming. You have to dedicate and devise the affirmation for yourself.

As with tattoos, thought and volition and personal taste must be addressed. Employ fragments from your favourite book, film or song. I can suggest, of course, the particles I recovered for myself. However, I rather suspect you need to concoct your own. Appropriate appropriately.

The things one collects, the objects and articles and remnants from pop or high culture one prizes, can offer great solace. I was recently reminded of this by a Walter Benjamin essay called 'Unpacking My Library' which a friend suggested I read when I was moving my own book collection. I had asked this person, who has a particular interest in Teutonic-type philosophy, 'Why am I getting off on reorganising my books so much? Am I, like, some materialist capitalist object-fetishising pig dog?' Fortunately, this bloke said that no, I wasn't, I was merely revelling in the anarchy of memories. Well, jolly good. Hate to be a capitalist object-fetishising pig dog. Benjamin asserts that we build a dwelling of the artefacts and things we adore and disappear within them. That our precious bits and pieces, in all their chaos, can confer upon us a sense of order and comfort. Even if one does not 'collect' in the usual way, we all have a little store of favourite things. Attend this depository at once and procure preferred items and turn them into one of those affirmation things.

I am a bit suspicious of acquiring those Louise Hay type affirmations. Not only because I think her books are shite and she couldn't write her own name in the fucking sand with a stick, but because we NEED to exercise some volition in these matters. A personalised affirmation is a lot like making collage art. Or sampling. Or postmodern novels. Or whatever. Re-signing things, cutting things up, recontextualising them. The architect (you), the author of the affirmation, demonstrates to him/herself that things CAN be reorganised in a pleasing way. In a mode that suggests and is at 'peace' with chaos even as it gestures toward the skill of you, the connector. (Some of you theory-heads might intone at this point 'But Helen, the connector is dead. The author has been murdered. Didn't you ever bother to read Roland Barthes?' Well, yes I did. Mostly because I think *Writing Degree Zero* is the sexiest and punk-rockest title for a book ever. But, fair cop, you crazy postmoderns. I am not yet prepared to loosen the contours of authorship or identity. Let us just let the subject, the 'I' exist for a little while. Until, say, the year

Gas *Smells* Awful

2003, or until you and I have grappled properly with this entire depression and anxiety palaver. Okay? Call me old-fashioned. I bloody am. I only just discovered electronic trance, for Goddess's sake. What a loser. So I have NO hope of evincing subjective infinitude, trajectivity or whatever you want to call it.) Pinching stuff and making it pretty is good for your health. Rhyming and stealing, as the Beasties might put it.

One of my best girl friends (Shite, one is assuming the guise of a profoundly social and popular monster. This is not the case. Be assured, I hardly have any friends at all!) has discussed the benefits of this theft and re-signing with me. A lot, actually! While I do my little stolen pop culture affirmations, she pops off to antique markets to look at, or purchase if funds allow, old handbags. And she absorbs them, takes them home, rearranges them, puts them in the context of her other handbags. Her cute little bags have become a form of pastiche and relaxation. An exhibition. A laboratory even! The handbag habit appears to be an innocent (if faintly obsessive) one. However, I think it's quite clever and complex. I believe she is a freelance textile curator and active art historian, and I imagine my learned friend pottering about and reassembling her velvet, vinyl, calico and rayon acetate containers and it pleases me. As I am certain that she derives a particular, if ephemeral, kind of peace as she addresses her museum and says something to herself about the shape of the world. And, further, if one wishes to extrapolate, probably something about the nature of femininity also. And about potential and secrets. What is IN those handbags after all? And what does it mean that most of them are EMPTY? I think it is so cool that she has a handbag habit. I think it is so cool that she 'borrows' or steals this girlie artefact and takes it to an hilarious extreme. I like the way she pinches stuff and reorganises it. I mean, NO WAY was any one woman SUPPOSED to have that many handbags! She removes the handbag from its original context. She takes the piss. And it makes her feel better. And it warms my clouded, brittle, tepid little heart to see my friend content.

Actually, most of my loony co-conspirators evince some form of productive theft. The consensus is that shoplifting 'culture' provides relief. And although some of us ('us' is Helen and her five or so friends) actually MAKE MONEY out of our appropriation, we acknowledge that the reason we started doing it in the first place was out of a desire for mental health. Making fun of adverts in the lounge room, DJ-ing, dressing in drag, everyday parody, cutting up text, even bloody changing an ingredient in a recipe are all things that can calm us down a little. I have noted that my mum changes the placement of photographs when she's a little tetchy. My dad does data entry on his self-devised horse racing software. My sister might obsess about the quality of a roux for hours. I rearrange the personal minutiae on my refrigerator. (It is funny that the fridge has become the frame for my reassembled unease, I think.) Further, my flatmate Jen brought one of those little blackboards with her when she moved in. Lately I've been going through this unctuous Paul Virilio phase and writing things about generalised interactivity and derailment on it between words like 'toilet paper', 'wanky balsamic vinegar to impress house guests' and 'pay the fucking phone bill, Helen'. And I also inscribe funny things I've heard on it. Like I was in Acland Street the other day and this tufty subculture person who was sharing my table said 'excellent spliffage' from within his THC fug. The redundant suffix 'age' made me laugh so hard, up it went on the board. Sure, Jen thinks I'm a nut. I think she kind of knew that when she moved in, though. And I rather assume that she suspects all this mindless, silly theft and replacement provides the substructure for my sanity.

Oh, and of course, the net is a great and convenient and portable locus for burglary. You can download bits, change your desktop picture and forge your own inimitable narrative with hyperlinks. (I am certain I will blather lavishly about that hyper shite later, though.) Anything that is a little bit mindless and a little bit reconstruction, really. A little bit country and a little bit rock and roll.

So, overtly I've trailed away in all my errant trajectivity on this appropriation jag. And I do this not to instruct you to issue forth this instant and become some dada art weirdo. (Although, please do so if fancy strikes.) Just adhere to this process for your affirmations. And perhaps carry the notion of theft with you whenever you can. Because it is soothing at times to chew up the world, digest it and then vomit the residue up in an 'acceptable' or intriguing way.

So, as to my own affirmations. Oh, fuck that. Let us begin to call them appropriations. What the hell. I love a neologism. These are offered merely to get you started if you are having trouble.

Helen's Appropriations: I'm an old-fashioned dialectical reasoning Marxist type with anarcho-punk proclivities. So The Clash worked very well for me. 'I'm Lost In The Supermarket. Can no longer shop happily' is a fragment I adore. Often followed by the Butthole Surfers' 'I got a stiff upper lip because I'm half dead. The walls of my life are crumbling around me.' Then I generally laugh, at my own unabashed pathos. Which I think is cool, you know. If Gibby from the Buttholes has not made me laugh at this juncture, I generally segue into some Sylvia Plath. Occasionally, as in certain filaments of the poem 'Lady Lazarus', she is uplifting. Mostly, however, I just read bits of her verse out because it makes me seem like such a teenager. And I have to laugh at my own blank irony and callow self-regard. The little stolen axioms might change from day to day. I try to impose some kind of linear 'progress' on them, I suppose. I try to make the apparently noncontiguous bits 'talk' to each other. Cos, apart from affording me a small sense of power and volition, at least it means I've actually done something that day.

I should be naked here and inform you that, very often, I afford my self-panic cessation with some Barbra Streisand. Because I LOVE Babs. And, after all, people who need people ARE the luckiest people in the world. Further, on a clear day you *can* see forever. Currently, the *Trip Reset* record from Psychic TV is working very nicely. And the book *Postmodern Fables* by Jean Francois Lyotard. And, always, quotes from Patsy and Edina and their comrades the Pet Shop Boys. The refrain 'just when you least expect it, just what you least expect' from 'Love Comes Quickly' thrills me to my putamen. (Yes, I know I am not a stone fruit and I have no essence. But I like the word putamen. And I think it is important for neurotics like us to like words and the difficulties and confluence and possibilities they may create.) Also, I will quite often get my battle-worn copy of *Catcher in the Rye* out just to take the piss out of myself, to 'be' Holden Caulfield for a minute or two. That usually sorts me. I am so repelled by my ability to become an isomer for Holden that I rush toward my version of maturity in fright. I talk like Holden and as soon as the words form in my mouth, they turn to dust. I shift from paralysis to embarrassed motility in a second. I think 'Oh Helen, even YOU are not that trite!' Salinger probably did not intend for his pusillanimous creature to be so expropriated. However, I feel certain that he wouldn't mind that his blank rebel bludgeons my own blank rebellion into submission. I Am Holden Caulfield. As soon as I acknowledge that I am, I am not. In the instant of achieving intimate proximity to this mutable and omniscient literary contrivance, I become something quite other than Holden. I accede to Holden. I yield to his presence, take on his form and, in so doing, interrupt my self-destructive Holden-ness. I allow this prevalent, dysthymic character to seduce me. I engage with him so that I may then disengage. I desire Holden, I get him and then I just don't want him any more. Phew.

Upon the (profoundly) odd occasion, I will also randomly flit about the marketplace of ideas and 'culture'. I will just open the *New Weekly* and see if I can conjure any sense from it. (Shite, I'm a nana.) You know, sometimes the truth does inhere in an article about Tea Leone's morphing bra size. Well, she is adjacent to David Duchovny, so I suppose truth is commonplace for her.

At my most destabilised I would often perform an earthy melange of corporate lager commercial jingles to a captive audience of next door's unconscious cat. You know, if I was singing beer ads, I wouldn't seem like I was taking it seriously. These bloody affirmation things do have a habit of working, humiliating as that is to impart. So do like I do and make fun of yourself. Try some parody or pastiche in your affirmation. This was mine: I Can Feel A Hiss Fit Coming On. I Can Feel A Seizure Coming On. Just Can't Wait For

It. Got The Taste For It. I Can Feel A Nervie Coming On. You Can Get It Working A Plough. You Can Get It Milking A Cow. As A Matter Of Fact, I've Got It Now. Panic. Incendiary, Ice Filtered Fear. Have A Cold Gold Funny Turn. Refreshing. Australian. A Secret Recipe Passed Down Through The Generations. At The End Of A Long Day, There's Nothing Better Than An Effervescent Tall Glass Of The Fugue State. Et cetera.

Affirmations can sort of work if you devise the right style. It is a matter of debugging your poor old central processing unit. It is like Y2K is gonna happen, man, and you're an IT consultant and you're deciphering and rewriting the trillions of lines of bad code, baby. Yeah, do that crazy affirmation thing. Tell yourself that it is cool to be a fruitloop. That you don't NEED a reason. Re-sign pop culture. Re-sign everything. Re-sign yourself.

Chapter *Three*

Well, Miss High and Mighty, How do I Stop Crying About my Potty Training Quite So Much?

WELL, THAT'S PRETTY MUCH UP to you, smart britches. Not much help, am I? If it isn't obvious, I heartily recommend engaging the services of a therapist at once. I understand the manifold objections certain subjects have to the entire discipline. With very good, formidable reason. Again, I speak UTTERLY from my own delimited perspective. A shrink helped me greatly, is all. So maybe get yourself one.

This, of course, is an incredibly silly thing for me to demand of you so casually. The reality of shrink-location is far more stinking and problematic than I ever imagined. You just can't seem to get good help these days. Well, as it happens, you can, and I did, but it may very well be a long haul for you. Prepare to sit in six or seven or dickety million offices before you settle on a worthwhile employee. One rarely is satisfied with the first shrinko. Employing the correct psychiatrist or counsellor is an exhausting process. What do those noisome Americans squeal at the advent of such realisations? I believe it is Reality Check. Well, yes, we need one of those.

HELEN RAZER

LET'S GO SHOPPING FOR A SHRINK

You have to find someone you like and trust. I know plenty of people who have visited more than ten different therapists in their quest for some state resembling peace. Your authoress is one of those choosy people, actually. It is not every shrink or hirsute guru or shonky counsellor who can quiet that troublesome internal din. Some of them are just plain awful. Some of them, I reckon, can actually retard your recovery. Sadly, stupid idiot therapists are just a fact of life. What do we look for? What should inspire us with confidence? Should we trust our abundantly shredded instinct? How much bratty precious trenchant nit-picking is permitted when we are shopping for our saviour?

Well, if like me you can waste an entire afternoon choosing the right shade of gun-metal grey mules and still not buy them, be as choosy as you like, I reckon. Don't settle for anything inferior. Okay? There are so many things of which to be wary. Be careful. Be vigilant. For a time all your energies are going to have to be heaped and employed for the task of finding a god-damn decent shrink!

Use your antennae. Trust your instincts, no matter how warped they presently are! Get someone decent and friendly. And ask questions. If there is a loony in your family or a rarely visited aunt who is renowned for her funny turns, demand the telephone number of their specialist. Do a net search, using the key words Oh Please Goddess When Will This Rude Torment End? Ha. No, I suggest going to health in the Yahoo search engine, actually. Read stuff. Contact fellow fruitbats. Research! For heaven's sake, some folks spend more time researching the credentials of practitioners of facials, decoupage and the correct use of a five iron than they do checking out their shrink.

The minimum requirements when therapist shopping are, possibly, as follows:

- Ask yourself, would I urinate on this person if they were aflame? If the answer is a resounding NO, go back to the crusty old GP and ask for a new referral. If you answered yes, make another appointment and see how things pan out. Honestly, it is important that you don't hate the bejesus out of your head-doctor. I mean, you may not want to bear his/her children. However, if on a purely visceral level you just don't like your therapist's smell, stay away. Genuinely. If you can't envisage yourself having a midway pleasant latte and chat with this person, strike them off the list. Who amongst us would take advice and restructuring from someone we loathe?

Quite naturally your intimates may revert to assiduous and orthodox respect for the medical profession and say, 'Oh golly gosh, you naughty minx, just accept that a person of his/her standing and education in life can help you!'. Crap. Psychiatry is one part science and ninety million parts art and instinct and manners. You need to see a bloke or a woman you actually respect. Tell people to fuck off when they insist that any dickwit with a cereal-box degree can assist you. You need to dig your shrink. Honestly. Legitimate tertiary qualifications provide no guarantee that you will be shriven, saved and generally improved. Be fussy, okay? This person could be giving you the raw materials to save your life. (The whole life saving thing—sorry, but it has to be said—is your responsibility in the end.) Be a little fond of your shrink. You don't want to dread seeing them.

- Has he or she offered you Rohipnol, Lithium and a place on an academic drug trial within thirty seconds of your first meeting? Yes? Oh dear. Check the Yellow Pages. Again. Yes, you may reason, your luck continues to sour! You have managed to encounter one of those indolent creeps who clings tenaciously to the antiquated notion that the human mind is a knowable, quantifiable mass. I have heard of head shrinkers prescribing after a mere three minutes of consultation. Well, obviously if you fall onto the couch screaming, 'I hate myself and I want to die, in fact I'm going to do it right now, doctor boy, just watch me hold my breath and tell my fucken parents I wish they were dead too', a therapist may be excused for force-feeding you Prozac.

Drugs alone are just not going to fix you up. No way. So be warned of the liberal pill-profferer. Oh, let me bore you with this demiofficial health warning again. Please be fucking circumspect where drugs are concerned.

Patently I can only impart advice from personal experience, but my shrink was excellent and he did not prescribe until I had attended several sessions. Not only did he wish to assess me for potential responsiveness to Selective Serotonin Re-uptake Inhibitors, but he waited to determine my own reaction to the notion of taking brain medicine. You may be one of those rare anxious souls who finds the thought of drugs repugnant. If this is the case, you need a decent shrink to assist you in making a responsible and informed decision. Cognititive Behaviour Therapy

Gas *Smells* Awful

is one option I know a little about. Beyond its effectiveness! Its genealogy can be traced to Thingummy Pavlov and his salivating canine. From the analysand's chair, it seems as though the therapist strives to bring on symptoms and assist the patient in micromanaging them. I would encounter my anxiety, distress and depression in a controlled environment and use or adapt a preexisting method of stemming their (seemingly) relentless flow. Basically it is about accelerating the development of novel and healthy responses to illness. It is like deciphering and reprogramming yourself. It is also referred to as desensitisation therapy. But if what you're offered is all chemicals and no talking or cognitive behaviour style cure, get out of there. A shrink armed with a multitude of solutions and perspectives is, generally speaking, a bloody good one. Stay away from those who vehemently believe in the powers of drugs ALONE.

Alternatively, you may be one of those 'give me pills' types, like me. I am very fortunate in having a doctor who knows when NOT to prescribe. Frankly, when depressed, I am likely to throw any fucking thing down my cakehole. As one with the unenviable ability to imagine any number of little pills as apotropaic, I bloody need a sensible doctor. You do too; especially if, like me, you are so ruddy desperate you can imbue just about anything with the power to save you. You do not need a pusher. You do not require a therapist who believes in finite solutions. You should run furtively away if you find ANY suggestion made by your therapist unacceptable and untoward. Especially if that suggestion involves numbing you on chemicals to a deleterious degree. Be sensible. Be vigilant Oh, but do remain somewhat open-minded. And don't take fucking drugs willy nilly. And that means pot and lager too.

- Are you unduly and negatively affected by the tasteless décor in your therapist's consultation rooms? I am cognisant that this sounds silly, but I know absolutely that I could never HEAL, baby, in a practice that boasted accoutrements such as quartz whale statuettes, op art or Elle MacPherson calendars. It is likely that I will restate this fatuous aphorism later: maintain your style. Hold onto your mode, your taste and your proclivities for nice little knick-knacks. These aesthetic preferences remind you that you are, in fact, still yourself. Your style is your point of difference. These little points of difference etch out the template of self. (I think Jacques Bloody Impenetrable Derrida has something to say about this in *Writing and Difference*. Which I reread last year when I was nutso. Not that I could fucking understand a word in my state! Maybe you'll do better.) Embrace your style. Coddle your difference. Attempt to surround yourself with meaningful, beautiful and resonant objects and things. And also, you have to be confident that your doctor is a nice person who you might choose to hang with were circumstances different. Soft porn or motel art on the walls have always been a good index, for me at least, that mutual respect is unattainable. I knew I was home, psychotherapeutically speaking, when I spied arum lilies in an alcove on a subtly lit cream wall, a bust of Friedrich Nietzsche and a huge pile of *Vanity Fair* back issues. Conversely, I ran puce and screaming from a North Shore practice when I saw chintz apricot sofas, muted lipstick on the too-pretty female receptionist, and *Architectural Digest* on the occasional fucking table. What therapist in his or her right mind would place this kind of noxious swill in a waiting room putatively appointed to calm down angry bitches like me? I don't want elitist reading matter gesturing toward the fact that my house is furnished with ugly shite items! The absolute LAST thing I want to see when I'm scattered and all at sixes and sevens is printed evidence of some rich fucker's perfect pastel granite benchtop life. This shit is important to me.

If, like me, you are easily mutated by your environment, choose a stylish practice. If you don't like the incidental reading matter, run! Further, I suggest that a bountiful display of novelty items from drug companies should be met with suspicion and disdain. Cheesy Zoloft executive toys and Avorax stress balls should NOT be on display. And a Deepak Chopra book within a five-kilometre radius of the joint should be treated as a harbinger of naught but psychotherapeutic doom.

- Is your new loving friend judgmental about your 'unconventional' lifestyle choices? Patently, if they humbly suggest that you might want to stop cutting your legs with a razorblade, or at the very least invest in a quality antiseptic lotion, then they are just being nice. If, however, they reprimand you for being an angry feminist or they try to cure your homosexuality, phone some sort of shrink watchdog and get the fuck out. If a psychiatrist has a political or ethical motivation rather than an impartial one, he or she ain't gonna do you any good any time soon. You don't want to inherit somebody else's counterfeit version of mental health. You want one that works for you and addresses your specific needs and style. A good shrink should refrain from proselytising. (I was aghast when I visited a consulting psychiatrist and his first question was 'Are You Married?' What? Hello? What kind of fucking late millennial interrogatory is that supposed to fucking constitute? No, I am not married and I don't think I ever fucking will be because I can't, after many years of assiduous thought, see the fucking point in marriage. 'Do you have a partner?' or 'Describe your closest relationships to me' would have been infinitely preferable to this heirloom of a psychiatric inquest! Such a question presumes that (a) I am the sort of person who would accede to an orthodox betrothal (which I don't think I bloody am); (b) I am heterosexual (The entire NOTION of any kind of 'sexual identity' leaves me replete with rage. Gay, lezzo, straight, bi is all a load of old shite. I fucking refuse to 'identify'. Let us all be queer, please); and (c) that I presuppose, as he so obviously fucking does, that a cosy cohabiting straight love arrangement is the corollary of mental health. Which it is fucking not! (Hey, it is simultaneously possible to be single and sane, you know! Conversely, it is possible to be married and unhappy and unstuck. Fuck him, I thought. So, I pissed off quick.) You may not be a total leftie pinko trousers like me. You may have a thoroughly different world view. If you do, overtly you are notionally broken and wrong, for Helen Is The Way And The Truth (joke haaa). Seriously, kids, even if you have a world view that is markedly different from mine (and remember, I am thoroughly correct in all of my thinking. Tee hee.) your psychiatrist should not try to amend it. A leftish shrinky friend of mine related a

Gas *Smells* Awful

story to me recently. My bud, the doctor type, was confronted with a virulently racist little motherfucker of a patient. Although she was, frankly, repulsed by her patient's perspective, she went to great pains to conceal this. As she jolly well should have really. As tempted as this girlie doctor was to indicate that the patient's own experience of hardship and oppression and prejudice was really analogous to that of the black persons her patient despised, she did not. Good on her. It was none of her business really. Avoid shrinks who tell you how to live and think. You've got to devise those things on your own. (Even if you are a probity-deficient right-wing xenophobic fuckstick! Yeah, they have feelings too, I've heard.)

Oh, another prevalent problem with therapists (quite apart from frequent and elephantine stupidity, of course) is their allegiance to a particular 'cause'. I have had a number of female acquaintances, for example, tell of their experience with counsellors who remain convinced that their patient's malady is the result of forgotten sexual abuse. While this ineffable, repulsive, cut-the-assailant's-dirty-little-prick-off-with-rusty-shears-and-feed-it-to-wild-bushpigs-and-put-it-on-primetime-network-commercial-television crime is heart breakingly common, it doesn't always happen to everyone. Just watch out for One Solution Fits All doctors. Further, there still exist some Freudian traditionalists who actually believe that the entire feminine gender has never evacuated the process of mutual absorption and indistinct identity that occurs during breastfeeding. They think that all ladies are sort of half-formed men. And there are those creative type therapists who wish to turn us all into artistes. Like, why the fuck should a really proficient and talented plumber have to draw free intuitive pastels of bloody happy goats or something? Just avoid fuckwits who are too opinionated and lazy to think, essentially.

- Finally, do you suspect that this person can really help you? Will they consider an alternative course of treatment if, for example, the talking cure is not the thing for you? When you ask questions about the reported efficacy or history of a certain kind of therapy, can they answer you readily? Regarding this last point: personally, my shrink favours a desensitisation therapy called EMDR. (If you want to check it out, the URL is www.emdr.com). This works fine for me, I'm really not a talking cure kind of girl. (I have noted that total blabbermouth, lexically obsessed folks such as I often respond better to a relatively taciturn style of treatment. Some of us just don't need to do any more fucking talking. However, you silent types might want to consider talking your way out of distress.) We chatted about this extensively and I knew I was with a decent shrink when he gave me truckloads of books to take home and some useful URLs. We might be fragile dribbling beasts, but sometimes we do need a bit of intellectual coddling, don't you think? The fact that you are incapable of buying the milk without shaking uncontrollably should not necessarily preclude the possibility of your learning something about cognitive behaviour therapy, or Lacanian neo-Freudianism, or whatever else tickles your ailing fancy. (Oh, but if you don't give too much of a crap, I wouldn't worry.)

Find a therapist who involves you in your cure. Do not select an analyst who makes things easy for you. You need a writerly cure!

Gas *Smells* Awful

That is, you need to assume the demeanour of a very clever and diligent literary critic when reading the text of your life. If you find that your therapist is trying to render the narrative of your dysfunction into some egregious Mills and Boon pulp when what you really have before you is *Voss*, *Wuthering Heights* or *Ulysses*, then scram! Find a shrink who makes you work. 'Tis better, after all, to do the strenuous shit in a comfy office chair than on the bus to work.

So, like your shrink. Trust your shrink not to put you in a stupefying drug-induced membrane. Approve of your shrink's taste in interior design. Ensure that dialogue between you and shrinky occurs in an ethical vacuum. Know that your shrink can write her/his name in the sand with a fucking stick. In essence, if you are able, be guided toward a decision by your instinct.

Oh, and, if you can bear it, please be assured that psychiatry is a *reasonably* evolved art and that partial or decent or excellent help is at hand. And that if you are currently being tormented by a total quack, you will eventually unearth the most suitable and adept belfry technician. There is hope. Balance is attainable.

But when engaging the services of a head-doc, there's a whole mound of other stuff of which to be terribly wary. We should remember, of course, that therapy costs a lot. You might want to consider actually seeing a proper shrink with alphabet soup letters after his or her name, because at least you get most of the dosh back on Medicare. There are a few nice doctors who have a sort of sliding scale arrangement. And there are even some good ones who offer bulk-billing to those in need. Further, if you can prove you had your 'injury' at work (or on the way there or back), you may get entirely compensated for it. (And kids, I'm not advising that you shiatsu massage the system here. There's a lot of folk who have a profound need for compensation. So don't bugger off with insurance claims you don't deserve. However, as I have learnt from experience, the workplace can be fraught with danger. Obviously, stalking is kind of my 'thing' but I did receive at least three hundred letters from Australian women, and a few men, who had been pursued by nutters in their ostensibly sober and composed and safe places of employment. So, just know that you may be entitled to some form of compo. Sometimes a girl or boy absolutely needs it! NEVER abuse compensation. Do, however, be apprised of your rights. See a lawyer if needs be, and talk long and earnestly to your human resources officer or equivalent if appropriate.) Students are generally entitled to avail themselves of campus counsellors or doctors at no cost. Occasionally high school students are permitted to use these same facilities. (Let us unwillingly confront the bleak reality, oh dysthymic adolescents. Most school counsellors are utter hippy shite! Sometimes it is a sensible idea to pursue more competent assistance.)

As the oft-egested nanna homily proceeds, 'hope for the best and prepare for the worst'. A lot of people ratified as carers are shite. But one must keep trying! Do not be surprised when confronted with punitive thugs or innocuous wimps. However, develop a keen eye for the legitimately therapeutic.

I must note that lots of you are shrinkaphobic. Very odd, this phobia, from my self-involved standpoint! You see, I always begged my mother as a youngster to send me to ANY kind of therapist. (Then again, I have always found myself endlessly fascinating. Even depressives are capable of the most prodigious self-regard!) You may be one of those selfless, I-don't-want-to-be-a-burden bods. Well, frankly, if you are incontinent with anxiety or you are only sleeping for three minutes a night or you're frightened of fish, being a burden is the least of your worries. Just get over yourself and make an appointment.

In one recent terribly brave adventure, I actually had a serendipitous milkshake with an old school buddy in PUBLIC without my customary balaclava. Then a bloke who used to be in a band with my ex-best friend's brother showed up. Chatter, muse, ponder. All very nice. Then the lovely lass from high school tells me she has chronic irritable bowel syndrome featuring rectal bleeding as a result of anxiety, a propensity to shack up with men who pinch her money, and a monumental drinking problem. (Good luck to you, babe, you looked great despite it all!) And the rock boy spoke of paralysing anxiety attacks, unfathomable fear and immobilising depression. He'd even managed to fuck a potential recording contract because he couldn't perform the evening that the Artist and Repertoire guy had actually bothered to come and watch his band. Too busy thinking he was going to die backstage. He was on GP-prescribed Zoloft; she was seeing eighty-nine specialists, and when I offered them my shrink's number they both said, 'Oh don't worry, I'm not that sick!' What?

We'd all like to think that we can effectively perform our own psycho-therapeutic operations. That we are clever and objective enough to forge new synaptic pathways. That we are Nietzschean Over Men who are strong and infused with blokey will. Well, we're not. We're a bunch of really sad flaccid people! We need fucking help!! We need it yesterday! HAVE YOU MADE AN APPOINTMENT YET?

How often have you heard people (generally those in dire need of professional assistance) intone, 'Well, if I can't work it out by myself, it's not worth working out'? What? Hello? What kind of fucked-up logic is that? Why are we so averse to the notion of emotional guidance? What the fuck is wrong with us?

I am so amused when I read the notes from my initial therapy sessions. They are replete with trite rationalisations and lots of, 'Well, I don't really think I need to be here.' What? I was an insomniac, vomiting, shaking, blind-with-anxiety wreck. And I mean really blind. I actually couldn't see. And I still thought I was too clever for therapy and too strong for drugs. I didn't even take them for a while. I let them stay in their little silver envelope until I thought, 'Oh fuck it, in for a penny in for a pound' and I began eating them in prescribed doses. And I didn't allow myself to be suggestible and pliant in therapy for quite some time either. (Now I should impart that such a tactic is not necessarily bad. A little suspicion can be good. You should trust your therapist before you start telling them about the first time you vigorously affricated your genitalia or fetishised a cucumber or endured the primal scene or dreamt about being a beach ball or whatever. But, in the crass parlance of Australian public houses, there's a big difference between scratching your bum and tearing your arse to shreds. That is, there's a vast chasm between caution and total paranoia. Similarly, there's a continent between a robust suspicion of chemicals and irrational fear.) One does, eventually, have to open up in the manner of some noxious, overabundantly flowering stinkweed. Or a pretty fucking pink fucking tea rose, if you prefer.

Just go to the goddamn head doctor, will you? If nothing else, you will eventually see some poor person with obsessive-compulsive disorder wearing one shoe and whistling *'I've Never Been To Me'* repeatedly in the waiting room who will make you feel SO much better about yourself. (I am sorry. I know that it is not very nice to find succour and solace in other's comparative misfortune. But, on certain days, as long as you don't shit anyone too badly, whatever fucking works, no?)

So, we have established that it's fine and justifiable to be sick, that it's equally cool to be a temporarily selfish brat and that employing a shrink is essential. Haven't we done well? So, on to:

ELEMENTARY THERAPY PROBLEMS

When you have actually settled into a life that will be pretty much dominated by therapy, you will perhaps encounter a few other thorny, guilt-inspiring problems. I want to chronicle one or two of the annoying barriers I so ably (HA! YEAH! RIGHT!) thwarted.

Shrink Envy. You may well find that those closest to you, despite their best intentions, become envious of the time you are spending with your head-shrinker. (Chicks, I must impart, are particularly guilty of this. They just can't grasp WHY they cannot function as your very own big bouncy personal apothecary.) You are just going to have to pleasantly explain, between bouts of self-loathing, to your wannabe doctress or white-coated orderly that you love them to bits and pieces, but would they please fuck off and leave you alone with your therapy. Parents are also fairly adept at proffering prognosis, advice or home-made cures such as 'Why don't you just get out in the sunshine?' To which you naturally reply, after offering a treatise on the high incidence of melanoma, 'Sunshine? Birdies? Frigging Kitty Fucking Cats? Stick a knife in my heart, why don't you? Give me dim lighting, cup-a-soup and talk shows or give me death, you insidious horror!' Sad as it is, your therapist is going to become the most important person in your life for a time. Your friends, bonks and folks are just going to have to deal with the knowledge that their help, while vital, is secondary. If somebody likes you well enough to be miserable that they can't help you more, try to be flattered and emboldened rather than annoyed. And if your true love, mate or mummy *really* wants to help, maybe they could go and get you a nice pizza or something? Suggest that to them. Hawaiian, thanks. And a side order of DEATH, PESTILENCE AND TORMENT while you are about it. We'll talk later about tranquillising other folks' suspicions in detail. Other people, as previously mentioned, can be royal pains in the arse and they need their own chapter. So they'll get one. Stay tuned.

Transference. You may have heard of the phenomenon. I haven't bothered to study it in any great depth as I, touch wood, haven't had to deal with it as a patient. So, be assured, I wield the term with an absolute absence of authority! In any case, I think it has something to do with focusing hitherto repressed feelings on a new object, most often your shrinky. You may find that you get a little crush on your therapist, regardless of their gender, attention to personal hygiene or dress sense. While a quality therapist will be able to deflate your passions, you might find that it starts to piss off your beloved. You may be bounding home full of, shrinky said this, shrinky said that, shrinky has a lovely new tie and shrinky said I looked positively radiant today. Well, that would rub any normal person the wrong way. I'd advise just shutting up about shrinky. Preserve the odd intimacy that occurs between analyst and analysand. While I will be forever grateful to my doctor for helping me out of the pig pen of muddy self-loathing, I did try not to bang on too much about him at home. (Not that my cohabiter of the time would have listened anyway!)

Diagnosis. The other elementary therapy problem I had inhered in the very naming of my illness. (If you were wondering, I think they were Stress Disorder, Acute Anxiety Disorder, Typical Depression and Post-Traumatic Stress Syndrome.) I have noticed other patients react in two distinct ways when it comes to giving their problems a title. The first is a feeling of utter, unabashed relief. Despite all the media attention lavished on mental health, there are still many folks who don't know what a panic attack or a bout of depression is. They find themselves suddenly fearing their death and they have no clue why. So they then think well, I jolly well MUST be about to cark it. As a teenage Sylvia Plath fan and one who has loonies on both sides of the family, at least I had some fundamental understanding of the terrible things that were happening to me. (This by no means stopped me from fearing my own imminent demise! Even though I can now ably recognise the textbook symptoms of a panic attack, that lurid irrational part of me still plans ahead for the cremation and discerning wake wine list and canape menu. I want my mourners to drink cheap, peppery and young shiraz. So they wake up the next day with an intimation of how fucked up I truly was. Fuck, but I am a grown-up! Why don't I spend my idle anxious hours thinking about world peace or something?) A lot of you folks really think there is something critically wrong with your bodies, don't you? A lot of you have NO CLUE that it is your heads that need a-fixing. Obviously the realisation that your problem has a distinguished-sounding name AND a whole host of modalities ready and waiting to tackle it feels to some like an exotic gift. To others, like Miss Helen, a brand can be naught but anathema. As one who adores to believe in her own idiosyncratic preciousness, I was a little sore when my psychiatrist dared to tell me I had a common illness! As a pathological rebel and naughty upstart about town, it brought me down to think that I was so mundane I could be categorised. I was really looking forward to being featured in *Psychology Today* or the *Lancet*. I had hoped that psychopharmacology would be a fundamentally altered discipline when I appeared with my fabulously distinct new illness. No such luck.

Actually, what I did to exceed this bland misfortune was to invent my own special psychotherapeutic neologism. I had acquired, according to me, a very rare, special and complex phrenic distemper known as Van Pelt's Disorder. Named, of course, for the imperious Lucy Van Pelt from Peanuts. Although Snoopy pretty much shat me, Lucy Van Pelt was, and remains, my malcontent role model. The world needs more cruel Lucys! Well, possibly not. But it tickled me nonetheless when I told people that I had Van Pelt's disorder. They would look all concerned and intrigued when I invoked this fictitious ill. And I would imagine myself snatching their paltry little

Linus blankets and tripping them over relentlessly and kicking them in their adipose Charlie Brown arses. Tee hee. And I was content, in my wan twisted manner. I even considered getting a black and burnt orange zigzag dress made. I have too many problems to count. However, if you feel like claiming your illness and all its distinct subtleties, by all means give it a name. Call it Costanza-itis, after George from 'Seinfeld'. Or Bronte's Complaint. Or Plathsymia. Or say you are suffering from Cobainism. Dickenso-Mania for Emily. Rimbaudism. Hendrixonia. BrianJonesoria. Whatever. Invent your own little title. Language is power, as the structuralists said.

If you have a negative initial reaction to diagnosis, just ignore it. (Of course, if you hear the word 'bipolarity', that may be a little more difficult. However, even you folks who are deemed to have a congenital chemical imbalance, if there is such a bloody thing, can live a decent life.) In all cases, try to remember that we are not immutable beings. We are capable of propitious and fleet and impressive change!

Therapy Addiction. Do be careful of therapy addiction. I know people who are thoroughly seduced by the IDEA of therapy. In their desire for the Pure Idea, the essence of the process, they manage to extinguish the actual experience. Um, if you don't quite get me here, perhaps think about (a certain kind of) sex. You want it, you have it, you're doing it but, somehow, you're not engaged or present. (Or was that just me?) Many folk are just in the deepest kind of love with the idea of shrinkage. They become adept at 'revealing' themselves and simulating emotional nudity. They cloak themselves in a 'version' of nakedness. They are frozen in their desperation.

They cling to the style of the neurotic, if you see what I mean. I'm sure you do.

Just another thing of which to be leery.

I know it's all a savage pain in the date and that, in your condition, there are so many other things you'd rather be doing than chasing around for a good mental sawbones. You've just got to do it. BLOODY DO IT. Don't look at me like that! Get on the phone. Now. Sorry to sound like a notional Nike salesperson, but I don't know many nut-jobs who haven't accelerated their recovery by YEARS without seeing a doctor. You NEED someone to project-manage the reconstruction of your sad scattered remnants. Furthermore, you require the services of one who is inured to the challenge and the oddness. Shrinks are pretty comfy with us mad folks, generally speaking. As a rule they are not going to run screaming from the room when you tell them about your symptoms. They are not going to say, 'Hey, you're a fucking weirdo!' when you tell them that the wind makes you cry, that the colour purple makes you physically ill or that you have an abstruse terror of wooden pencil boxes. Or whatever.

You can't do it quite so effectively on your own. You cannot 'control' yourself. You need to rebuild yourself. Self-discipline is a crock where anxiety and depression are concerned. You might just need someone else to take over. And if you are the hair-shirt type—which I, quintessential lazy-bones, am most certainly not—don't underestimate the strength you will need while undergoing therapy. You will STILL have your pain. I vow! You will still face virtually insurmountable obstacles. Dear masochists, the great thing about therapy and its concomitant period of accelerated recovery is that

Gas *Smells* Awful

you can look forward to a HUGE amount of pain and suffering all at once! Yes, why endure years of indeterminate dull pain when you can wrestle with the incisive cruelty of a rapid healing process? Don't think therapy makes it easier. It's just that the therapeutic route can, quite simply, prove more direct and efficient.

In short, find your shrinky, treat your poor bonce with respect and prepare for a cavalcade of fabulous new symptoms.

Oh, and (like it matters!) you still have my unfettered respect if you choose not to 'see someone'. (This phrase amuses the crap out of me. So many people I know are in, or are in need of, therapy. So in my cosseted little realm, the interrogatory 'Is she seeing anyone?' has now transmuted from meaning 'Does she have a bonk?' to 'Has she got a doctor?' This shift makes me giggle.) I am certain you have good and well-structured reasons for not seeing a doctor. I have no will to be some didactic nightmare woman and INSIST that you see a shrinky AT ONCE. I am confident that you can articulate and chart the route that led to your choice of 'going it alone' etc. Um, but if you can't, you may wish to reassess your decision, okay? Just for me. Please.

Chapter *Four*

Well, Miss Self-Appointed Noodle Clinician, I'm Seeing a Shrinky, So Why am I Feeling Worse?

THE REALLY CRAP THING ABOUT therapy and getting better in general is that it hurts quite a bit. It really ripped my bib when I found that out. The other annoying feature of de-loony-ising oneself is that the ascent to relative sanity is jagged. You take what you assume to be a momentous step forward and then there you are crying, shrieking, hyperventilating, vomiting or overdosing again. Apparently all kinds of recovery from illness take this form, so prepare yourself for the one-step-forward-two-steps-back paradigm for a while.

I have been reliably informed by a league-playing and neurotic acquaintance of mine that a football leg injury will heal in a similar desultory fashion. One can attend the gym, take costly vitamins, stay off the blasted thing and make ostensibly fabulous progress. Then one day, for no apparent reason, the buggery bollocks knee will pack up on you again. Just when you fucking DON'T need it most. Just when a field goal is about to save the game. In time the leg may heal rather nicely. But it is an unctuously long road. Moreover, the rugby league playing bloke can still feel a twinge now and then. (The formerly fractured pin can become a fairly good index of rain!)

Apart from the simple fact of good old-fashioned muscular wear and tear, the actual *process* of recovery from your football injuries is going to change you irreversibly. The manner in which you approach your injury (or illness) will, in many cases, impact upon you in the long term EVEN MORE FORCIBLY than the injury itself.

My acquaintance reckons that throughout the healing process he actually learnt to do things differently. He favoured the other leg and he employed new hitherto untried and unflexed muscles. He is still pissed off about the injury. And, as a fit and active and brawny high-metabolism sort of bloke, he didn't really enjoy all the time he spent on his back. However, he's obviously fond of his new barometric skills and he's proud of the fact that he recovered to the extent that he's back to playing footy. Albeit evincing a slightly different on-field style. Actually, when he had a few beers one evening, he told me, in an uncharacteristically fatalist mode, that the injury was meant to happen. 'I'd Have Fucking Killed Myself On The Field If That Buggery Bollocks Injury Hadn't Slowed Me Down' were, I believe, his lager-sodden words. There followed a long period, needless to impart, of Helen proselytising and analogising and saying 'Oh Woe Is Me' about her anxiety and depression. And then I found out that he had been, at one time, even loonier than I ever was. (Nothing directly to do with his leg injury. He was just another nut-bar.) So I shut the fuck up and bought dickety hundred rounds as recompense. Whatever. At some point we attained accord and decided that recovery from lunacy is painful and transformative and problematic. But probably worth it all in the end. We just have to be careful when tackling. Anything, really.

Gas *Smells* Awful

If you have not already noticed that your early progress is seemingly impeded by doubt and FABULOUS new symptoms, get used to that thought now. SHIT WILL KEEP HAPPENING. And strange fast shit. Worse shit. I have NO idea why this occurs. It simply constitutes a major pain in the date. What can one say? You can take your pills with religious and regular and ritual fervour, attend all your therapy sessions without fail, enact the prescribed breathing exercises AND stay away from caffeine and cigarettes and STILL suffer badly from the relentless and/or mutated return of your symptoms.

Recovery from anxiety and depression does not follow a linear and progressive path. It is undulating and painful and unpredictable. Recovery in itself is terrifying, irksome, costly and potentially harmful. (So is rugby league, if you ask me. Most especially post-Murdoch fuck up.) One should approach the matter of getting better with few expectations and a complete absence of judgment. Not only do anxiety and depression change you thoroughly in the short-term. The process of recuperation will itself transform you forever. It will touch and try your patience, your intellect and your ontological belief systems! It will alter you physically, as well as mentally and emotionally. It is a bloody difficult bloody thing this getting bloody well bloody business. It is not easy and, certainly, it is not without its damnably annoying byproducts.

The tricks my anxiety and depression would play upon me as I began in earnest to divest myself of them! I don't know whether my body and psyche evolved a type of homoeopathic model in order to make me better, but it often felt that way. It was as though I was frequently administering 'contained' doses of misery and fear to myself in order that I might eventually develop a relative immunity to such nastiness. You know, like a pox vaccine? Actually, I managed to get about six different bouts of true influenza in the season that coincided with my illness. And I have spoken to others who have accrued a similar catalogue of physical illnesses attendant to their mental maladies. During these occasions my flu would mime the symptoms of my anxiety and depression. You know, as flus tend to. Headaches, nonspecific pain, insomnia, narcoleptic episodes, loss of perspective—literally—and general physical confusion. The really odd thing was, when I recovered from each of my matches with physical illness, I'd almost feel relieved and strengthened. I mentioned this in therapy and it was my doctor who happened to mention the homoeopathic comparison. Patently, a lot of folks would say, 'Well, you were depressed. Of course your immune system was flawed and you caught everything going, you duffer! Stop this elaborate immunisation model crap!' However, I maintain that my body produced extreme physical symptoms because it needed to. First, my physical illnesses drew my attention away from my mental ones. My symptoms could be affixed to a point of origin. Very comforting. Oh yes. The reason that I feel like I'm going to die of pain is the flu! Cool. Second, I believe, rather ardently in fact, that my sad little blonde mass was synthesising immunity to future symptoms. My flus deadened my shock to anxiety and depression. Further, the scabrous nature of my proto-recovery period panic attacks and depressions had a purpose. Although these hurt like hell, they caused me to become more impassive and accepting. Sort of like electro-convulsive therapy, I suppose. (Although ECT sounds like a load of old shite, doesn't it? You know that they even do that to kiddies? In 1999!)

Gas *Smells* Awful

On occasion I felt confident that I had thwarted particular symptoms. One day I was positive I had cleverly exceeded the punishment of depersonalisation. (You know, that egregious feeling that you're simply not in your body. The sensation that you are rapidly unravelling. The suspicion that you have recently broken metaphoric wind beyond your control. You know that one? The diabolic nexus of depression and anxiety. Yes, her.) Well, on certain misguided occasions I was sure I had managed to rid myself of this putrescent beast. I was smug that I had remained in my body for close to an entire weekend! Then, blam! She grabbed me with alacrity and pure passion and ripped me out of my body further than I had ever ventured before. I was on the other side of the room. Although I had not physically moved, I could watch my perspective drain and transmute. The clock I had been staring at so forlornly now receded from view. I was yanked, thrashed about a bit and left in an inconsolable heap. These fits, or whatever one calls them, persisted for a matter of weeks. I have never reproduced kiddy brats (and probably never shall. Do I really want to bestow my pallid psychological imprint on some poor infant fucker? NO!) but I imagine that this sensation is similar to giving birth. The panic and fear and all-consuming blue electric misery animals taunted me for months, threatening to emerge. They had been bloody gestating. And in an act of primal cruelty, YANK they exited from my poor form and then accrued their own separate identity. What a fucking relief, in the end! After all those contractions and phantom labour scares. My demonic children, of course, continue to demand my attention. They have left me emotionally flabby and with an ungainly patina of stretch marks all over my psyche! And they still bother me from time to time, demanding costly orthodontic mindfulness, money for school excursions and my unimpeded concern. At least they are fucking out of me now, though. I loathe my bratty brood. And I think, needless to impart, frequently of infanticide. It's a bitch this postpartum depression depression. If you see what I mean.

So many things can get broken during the initial stages of therapy. Like lancing a pustulant boil, getting your stiches pulled out or waxing one's bikini line, however, the results of the agony are generally worth it.

Recovery from anxiety and depression in no way mimics the widely murmured suburban affirmation, Every Day In Every Way I'm Getting Better And Better. In manifold ways, you just get fucking worse.

For me, headaches were a massive problem. This probably had a little to do with the way I was holding my poor overburdened shoulders. However, I suspect (and there is no medical evidence, to my knowledge, to support this ludicrous hypothesis) that my brain was figuring out new ways to do things. New bloody synaptic pathways forming, or grumpy neural transmitters who'd got the shits with me taking off on an afternoon walk or something. I don't bloody know. If it isn't already abundantly obvious, I'm talking through my arse. Although I remain convinced that the headaches signified change.

I was chatting with a similarly depressed and anxious babe on the telephone only recently. Ground zero occurred for us around the same time. We sought the same kind of help, being similar disgruntled ladies and all, and we still manage to mirror the other's distress, fairly much. We expressed our horror at the panoply of symptoms and suspicions our poor minds continue to reproduce. We marvelled not only at the protracted nature of our illness but at the pain and difficulty incurred by our assiduous therapeutic reconstruction. We were aghast to discover that novel symptoms arrived on a near weekly basis.

'I mean, I am almost curious to discern what my brain will do to me next,' said my loony mate. 'I approach my moderate version of mental health then my innards find new and wonderful ways to rebel.'

Upon occasion I have shared my friend's amusement. Sometimes it is just plain fucking comic to watch what your body will do to you next.

I can't even begin to chronicle all the silly things that will happen to you when you begin on the path toward sanity. Apart from the ratshit headaches, I experienced this gross and particular dizziness. It was just as though I was ascending in a very fast lift some fifty floors or so. Except that my stomach became my head. And because I was convinced my stomach was, indeed, my head, I was unable to eat! I was terrified of throwing up. You may feel something like that. Or you may just endure the tiredness of an age. You may just want to go to bed. You may wish to pace endlessly, unable to quash your seemingly futile energy. All these symptoms may, or may not, emerge distinct from the symptoms of anxiety. They may just seem to be separate and not at all contiguous to your Little Problem with stress. You can Be Calm and suddenly your body is in the middle of a step class. Whatever the sad bloody case, be assured, therapy is going to nudge one or two or innumerable pretty bloody odd acts out of you.

Therapy accelerates your journey through a number of sensations and symptoms that are, possibly, predestined. That is, all the shitty and endlessly shifting things that happen to you in the first few months of therapy were probably going to happen to you anyway. Well, I like to think so anyway. (Helps me justify all those frozen months!) Without therapy, anxiety and depression can seem like quite torpid monsters. The 'progress' of these disorders may be painfully slow. Oddly, you can become better used to managing (or quashing and ignoring) your foes when there is no therapeutic intervention in your sphere. Anxiety and depression can remain fairly static for YEARS. If you leave them to reside in a state of relative immutability, you can, perhaps, learn better to cope with them. It's like screwing up your knee and avoiding physiotherapy really. You can learn how to walk while preserving the injury. And you know . . . the analogy is pretty fucking obvious. The longer you leave it, the harder it is to heal. Blah blah fucking blah. Sometimes it appears easier to maintain the buggered knee than to cure it. Therapy hurts worse than the undisturbed pain. Et cetera.

When trudging on your shitty knee through the putrescent molasses that is existence (oh dear, will I just fucking shut up and buy a new dress or something) with your new friends anxiety and depression as company, you're only having a crap time and operating, in all realms, at about .000001 per cent of your potential. (And you know, I think it would be nice if we could manage to careen about the world using around 12 per cent of available phrenic and physical resources and make some cool shit.)

A prodigiously impressive array of pain, deception and symptoms awaits you when you step into therapy for the very first time. Not only will you have to grapple with Gargantuan horror, fear and deepest melancholy, but you will have to steady yourself for the speed with which they appear in new guises.

It's a new kind of weird numbing panic attack one day. Fear of toothbrushes the next. Your perspective changes beyond your control. Further, individual symptoms may themselves speed up. That is, something that has been troubling you will return to ravage you in a more potent, ragged and quicker form. Just like my feeling of being pulled backwards out of myself. This was sort of happening to me anyway, pre-therapy. However, it happened by such tiny increments, I didn't really notice it. I could be sitting in the same spot for hours, and I'd suddenly acknowledge that 'I' had shifted in relation to the scene before me. As therapy began to thaw me out, this would happen with savagely increased speed. Watch out for this. It is very painful and scary, but it means that you are on your way to your version of stability.

If you are a boffin type, perhaps you'd like to think about this new rapidity in terms of fast-moving particles or the speed of light or something. Essentially, when things happen too fast, although it feels as though you are speeding up and relinquishing stability, you are, in fact, getting closer to stasis. The faster things move, the greater your proximity to peace. I promise! So ride your crazy symptomatic dispatches. They are a harbinger of your reconciliation with sanity and harmony. Yes, this is a flawed analogy. Structurally and ethically. But it worked for me at one time. So I proffer it to you for your consideration.

Another fucking twisted thing that happend to me was recovered memory. And a concomitant sense of dislocation within time.

(Actually, if this happens to you, can I suggest a quiet look at Carl Jung's *Memories, Dreams, Reflections*. I know Jung is a discredited dickhead in many circles. And for solid reasons too, as far as I can perceive. I mean, what is all this quasi-mystic we-are-all-fragments-of-the infinite-being shite anyway? And the mass unconscious, what the fuck is that supposed to be about? And all that spooky crap! However, Jung's compelling account of his infancy and the manner in which the shards of these early memories pierce the pellicle of his adulthood made so much sense to me. Just a thought. Indulge at your own risk and will. Do not hold the authoress responsible for any subsequent epiphanies or hissy fits.) I really began to feel unstuck within the space–time continuum. To say the very least. Often, I would remember a prelinguistic incident as though it had occurred only yesterday. And yet couldn't remember what I had eaten for breakfast that day. Lucid recollections of childhood or adolescent conversations returned to me frequently. Then I would dial a number and immediately forget who I was trying to call. One afternoon I clearly revisited the day my baby sister came home from hospital. Then I went to King Street for some prescription drugs and forgot my address. I felt the crunch of my three-year-old collarbone and tasted the breakfast cereal I had eaten twenty-six years ago. I couldn't spell my middle name. I saw the appearance of chicken pox on my skin. I traced the shape of a particular welt with my finger. I even recalled the morning on which I first grappled with the concept of time. I remember thinking, in my childish way, that it was just a powerful myth anyhow! Sometimes I would feel Scary Mary and Head-Job Heslop pull my pigtails exactly as they had in Year Seven. But do you think I could remember my fucking PIN number?

Sounds returned, fragments of text and vivid recollections of dreams that were nearly as old as I was. I tasted certain brands of biscuits that are no longer available. The first time I wore a dress. My initial encounter with tripe. My sister's blonde hair, my father's seventies moustache and my mother's 'curly perm' all stormed their way into my immediate consciousness. The present faded, the future was unthinkable and the past dominated my every move. I mean, nostalgia is one thing. A veritable barrage of seemingly innocuous images, however, is quite another.

You, dear patient, must become inured to this odd time hotchpotch. I haven't really devised a suitable hypothesis for the anxious and depressed person's capricious and malleable attitude to time. But I'll divulge what humiliating crap I have so far attempted anyway! I mean, how could I embarrass myself any more than I already have? Did I mention I developed a phobia about raspberry-scented soap? Bloody spatio-temporality. Bloody western chronocentrism. Bloody construction of self. In any case, Miss Helen's inchoate theory involving the disassembly of linear time as we have known it. Ah hum. The temporary nutter (that's you and me, baby) is necessarily compelled to unravel some fairly basic Western epistemic assumptions. The first, as indicated previously, is the notion that selves are knowable. We know, better than even the French postmodern psychoanalytic thinker or ANY bloody philosopher of subjectivity, that selves are not quantifiable. We have experienced first-hand the terrifying 'truth' of existence. We have lived Sartre's nausea. We have enacted Derrida's difference beyond our will or control. We have evinced the Nietzschean Will to Power. We are living flesh proof of Roland Barthes' dictum that a speaking subject never coincides with itself. For heaven's sake, we are dribbling all over the place!

Second, we instinctively know to abandon the orthodox notion of chronology. We begin, quite reasonably and justifiably, to doubt progression. We are absent in our own presence. We reside intimately in the past. We scurry about trying to make order and sense of the filaments of text and memory and sensation and childish longing that flap about us. We literally leak out of our own heads. We feel, as we recover, pain that is at once figurative and literal. A suggestion or a word can immediately leave its imprint on our anxious bodies. Our distress is written on the body. Our flesh becomes articulate. And all that other chic poststructuralist crap. Our memories and ourselves bleed everywhere. Of course we're going to stop believing in time. And, of course our short-term memory is going to become, temporarily, obsolete. If we exist in all time simultaneously, why should we privilege recent memory? I reckon that is why we can't remember why we went to the socks drawer. Even if it is clearly marked 'socks drawer' and is full of socks and you have no socks on and you really need some.

Our mutation is so rapid in the initial phases of therapy that we are forced to face huge epistemological questions. We must ask, with authentic concern, Do I Really Exist? We suspect that we do not. Or we fear that we are nine trillion different people. Or that we are unbound. We fear that we are the waste product of somebody else's reality mill. Or at least I did. Simply put, I felt like ooze. I felt as though I was excess. I assumed that the world and all the people in it were carved from a large undifferentiated lump. Everybody except me seemed to be endowed with a stable, fixed and rigid identity. I was pouring all over the place. I was, I reasoned, the stuff that was left over when the primordial mass was divided neatly into people, objects and ideas. I was offcuts. I was pet mince. I was the stuff they put into the meat pies you buy at the Sydney Football Stadium. The shite that goes into hot dog sausages. The paper that is so substandard that it is not allowed anywhere near the recycling bin. I was remnants. I was seconds. I was missing a button, or I had three arms. I was a sorry discount. I was something you'd buy for fifty cents at Clint's Crazy Bargains. And the purchase was so crap that you'd curse for wasting even that amount! I was planned obsolescence. I was futile. I was waste. I did not exist. I was a byproduct. I was a side-effect. I was effluent. I did not exist.

All, or none, of these thoughts may whack you over the head as you march reluctantly through the therapeutic process. Do I exist? What Is My Conceptual Shape? Is There A Foundation? When Will The Fucking Prozac Kick In? I suggest that it is reasonable to address these problematics with the same commitment and respect a scholar of philosophy might. Doubt about the nature of reality and subjecthood is not only reasonable, it's actually kind of cool. From the pre-Socratics to Renée Descartes to Jacques Derrida, thinking about the stuff from which the world is wrought has been considered a 'higher' occupation. It is not madness to ask Do I Exist? Is Reality A Sham? What Is Language? Am I, In Fact, Several Different People? Is The Notion Of A Fixed And Quantifiable Self Merely A Convenient Fallacy Invented To Keep People Buying Plywood Entertainment Centres? You are most decidedly not a fruitbat if you wrestle with any or all of these family-sized questions. You have simply, and magnificently, joined a long tradition of incendiary thinkers. In France you'd have your own talk show, a really cute bonk, free meals at Tour L'Argent and a band of sycophantic slaves hanging upon your every dark word.

No-one, to my knowledge, has yet devised suitable and sustainable answers to the Really Fucking Big Questions. They're still arguing about it all over at the Sorbonne. So give yourself a lovely elephant stamp rather than a hard time for thinking about such cumbersome issues. Michel Foucault would have been so very proud of you!

So, really, when viewed from a certain angle, the initial and difficult stages of therapy and recovery are educative. Insight forces itself upon you. Ideas come rushing toward you at maximum speed and, believe it or not, you may feel grateful for them in the future. Allow the gush of complex understandings to run unchecked. You are simply being clever.

I am ambivalently pleased by many of the things I learned. As the sort of girl who has long (and often indolently and affectedly) addressed manifold chunky epistemic questions, I now feel some intellectual relief. Like many people, I'm a bit of a lazy thinker, I suppose. Although I always nursed a tepid ambition to make some decisions about the structure of reality one distant day, there was always something to distract me. There was the banking, the accountant, the landlord, the broken coat hook or vodka martinis with a filament of lemon to divert my noble quest. I always meant to finish *Disseminations* and make some modest sense of the fucker. I genuinely intended to conquer de Saussure, Althusser and Lacan. I had promised to engage with Jameson, Levi Strauss and Julia Kristeva. I intended to actually read my first-year philosophy texts without the aid of cheat notes. Even boring old Spinoza. And that

Hume dotard. And snoozy Locke. And turdy Kant. And John Stuart I'm Such A Humanist Fuckwit Mill. And Heidegger, who has been taunting me for an age. And Husserl. Oh gosh, and bloody Virilio. And read Hegel properly and get my head around this dialectical reasoning thing, because really it is kind of simple, so I could then go and reread Marx and then postmodern antihumanist sort of leftie stuff. And quantum mechanics, too. Walter Benjamin, Malinowsky, Cixous. And some art history, for shit's sake. And there are all those countries that exist without the contours of political maps whose constituents are having a really shitty time. Like Kurdistan and Nagaland. That I know NOTHING about.

Naturally, I'm way too much of a pop-culture obsessive dunderhead to womanfully wrangle with such weighty monographs and facts. However, I did manage to read some but not all of the aforementioned thinkers and things. And when I approached them, at the nadir of my depression and at the most accelerated point of my psychotherapy, I found that I understood them better!

I had become, and remain to a delimited extent, authentically mesmerised by the Big Fucking Questions and issues. My new comprehension of and fascination with human discourse and identity bleeds consistently into all current endeavour. In attempting to reconstruct and stabilise my 'self' I became relatively learned about the conceptual shape of human identity and endeavour. For me, subtext was everywhere! And today I still see previously invisible marginal gloss scrawled upon my every exchange and act and utterance.

Although an ostensibly egoistic act, therapy may have the fascinating secondary effect of making you more excentric, less egocentric and more legitimately fascinated by and implicated in the order of the world and the things within it. Perception and improved intellectual tone are intriguing side-effects of the therapeutic process. I know! I know! It hurts so bad to have to confront such monumental questions. And one's conclusions, so very often, are naught but pure nihilism. However, I do think that you should be mighty chuffed with yourself when interrogating the very nature of reality. Even if, like me, the answers you concoct are insubstantial and apparently depressing, you should take pride. (I kind of decided that there was no first principle, final authority or foundation. I decided that God had died years ago, that faith in anything was a crock and that Channel Nine provided constant proof of the ethical and substantial absence at the core of so-called reality in continuing to produce such unmitigated shite as 'Australia's Funniest Home Video'). Be smug that some stinking force has propelled you into a high concept locale! Embellish your theories of existence. Hell, write a book or something! Feel happy that you don't have to endure complacent garden-variety thoughts any more.

You're smarter now. Take pride.

The body begins to 'know' these things as much as the mind. (You may, like me, begin to doubt that there is any 'meaningful' distinction between mind and body.) As one's emotional responses transmute at around mach five during therapy, so too does the body redress its imbalance perpetually. And generally gives you the shits! You thought that your physique had rebelled during your breakdown? Well, poor lamb, wait until you start therapy!

I recently reread Lewis Carroll's *Alice* books. I was reminded in therapy of Alice one afternoon when I shrieked, 'I'm telescoping!' I felt terribly small in one instant and terribly large in another. Oh gosh this is odd. I am becoming larger, but is this as large as I will become? I am becoming smaller, but relative to what? I have quite forgotten my 'original' size and shape. (For a great, totally head-fucking exegesis of Alice, check out Gilles Deleuze's *The Logic Of Sense*. Also, Irigaray gives a treatment in *This Sex Which Is Not One*.) I felt at war with my body. It was reeling off in manifold directions at once. But, with the temporality problem, I had also lost sight of 'once'.

I was just a big old mess really.

It is worth noting that physical problems seem to be a rather gendered affair. (Oh, boys. Fear not. I am not saying it is worse for girls. The opposite, sort of.) For women, I believe, the experience of sensing emotional pain and depression directly within the body is particularly resonant. Perhaps this phenomenon is the corollary of that antique principle which suggests that women are telluric and generally all messy and replete with yucky chunky bits and wild suppurations and breast milk and blood and rooted within their body; whilst men, by contrast, are able to attain a metaphysical state. (So my feminist Philosophy 101 teacher told me anyway.) Women are understood to be literal, while men are figurative. And if one chooses to accept my premise (Ain't no reason you got to, kids. The embrace of my bullshit philosophical meandering is NOT a prerequisite for mental health. Quite the opposite, probably.) one can understand, perhaps, why blokes more often succeed in killing themselves. Women are actually inured to an emotional and/or intellectual experience occurring in the body even as it occurs in the mind. For chicks, there is no Cartesian mind/body dualism. Masculine subjects, I reckon (and I talk to them often!), are even more at war within themselves than gals. Men find the physical reification of mental anguish harder to deal with. Women, by contrast, are quite adept at and used to accepting grief in a physical way. Men top themselves, annihilate their bodies, much more readily than women.

I AM NOT saying that biology is destiny! However, the socially marked body, as distinct from the 'natural' body, can make certain decisions for you. If you have a willy and a relatively flat chest, the world has already contained your destiny to a certain degree. Ditto for boozies and twat. Not only do people make assumptions about your character on your behalf if you happen to own a penis (or a 'lack' of a penis), but after three or four good years of assiduous and totally fucked-up socialisation on this our ailing planet, your body also begins to synthesise reality and meaning for you. I believe that the case is not, as many traditional feminists would have it, one where 'people make assumptions about the individual based on the mere physical fact of his or her gender'. I mean, shit yeah, of course they do. I just reckon it is a bit more complex than that. Bear with me. Or don't. (I don't care what you do, you insensitive bastards. My shrink listens to me! So there.) Whatever. What I am TRYING to say is this: bodies can manufacture meaning. We internalise the world. To the extent that we really feel things in our flesh. Grief, joy, desire. And, of course, anxiety and depression.

If this nonsense about the socially marked body interests you at all, I would like to suggest that you read Michel Foucault's history of incarceration and punishment, *Discipline and Punish*. Luce Irigaray, a Lacanian psychoanalyst and feminist scholar I turned to repeatedly throughout the course of my illness, has nominated a word for the socially marked body, as opposed to the physical one. She describes morphologies rather than bodies. I recommend reading *This Sex Which Is Not One*. The first book is better for boys and the second is best for ladies.

Whatever the case, it all gets a bit messy, doesn't it? One thing bleeds into the other. Truth blurs into fiction. Yesterday impinges on today. Mind conflates with body to the extent that we actually think that we are going to die from emotional pain. I don't bloody understand it! I just know that a lot of jangly confusing crap keeps on occurring as we amble on the slippery trajectory toward health. That we are simultaneously children and adults, imagined and real, past and present. This stuff, I INSIST, does bear thinking about. Otherwise I wouldn't have crapped on about it for such a long time.

Think about what is happening to you. Watch the dissolution. Try, if you feel able, to chronicle it. I managed to write myself a few letters. Most are just too bloody embarrassing to print. Yes, there's a lot of Led Zeppelin lyrics in them and terrible drawings! Oh, and a whole heap of really feculent self-devised poetry. Urgh! Maybe you'd like to have a go at this type of thing yourself.

Oh. I found this the other day. It was written just after I had entered therapy. It's a little bit whacked (Oh, surprise, not!). Maybe you will find it illuminating. Probably not. It is a letter to my anxiety and depression. What a fruit bowl am I?

Dear Helen's Anxiety and Depression
Perhaps there are certain things that do not tolerate the weight
of one's analysis. Perhaps all the religious whackos and
neomystic dolphin fondlers are correct. There are certain things

that defy description. There are monumental events and intimations that simply exceed speech or thought. Perhaps language and logic have evolved in such a way as to allow these gaps in expression and understanding. Perhaps I would simply shrivel up and die if I was able to gesture with confident precision to all that I encounter.

I have an excellent memory. I venture that I cannot recall a moment in my life which I could not capably express or represent. Even when I was two or three. Even when I was prelinguistic. I cannot remember a time that preceded language. I cannot remember an event for which I could not provide subtext or marginal gloss. Reality and appearance have always coincided for me. I have always been able to tell you exactly how and why I feel.

Now, however, speech, thought and logic all elude me and I am at a loss. The intimate links, or the mergence, I had so ably forged (with the assistance of my perfunctory reading of and fondness for postmodernism) between life and text, body and mind, reality and appearance have dissolved. At present, there is this monumental THING that encompasses me, claims me, taunts me and governs me. And I am unable to do anything with it! I cannot write about it adequately. I cannot situate it within a metaphor. I cannot find a reference to it in popular culture or poetry or anywhere. Damn!

I find that my firmly held assumptions are shaken. My former mode of explaining and measuring all things is broke.

Simply, I feel like an infant. I am, I feel sure, the child of whom I have no memory. I am all gaping inarticulate maw and sticky groping hands and empty growling stomach. I do not think. I am not governed by reason nor by reasonable need. I am, for the first time, led by thorough desire.

And it is all your fucking fault. So piss off. I have much better things to do with my time.
Yours truly,
Helen

Well, yeah. It is a bit hippy writing a letter to your fear, disenchantment and self-loathing, isn't it? However, some months after stuffing it away on the hard drive, I reread it. And it was sort of interesting. Don't you think it kind of sounds like a love letter? Well, the sort of love letter that a nutter like me might write anyway! (Probably goes a little way to explaining my appalling relationship record to date!) Definitely sounds like a love letter to me. Written by some yappy cow who is obviously involved with a bloke who is totally wrong for her. (Sound familiar, Helen??)

Maybe you should communicate with your recovery in this way. Write it a big old nasty letter replete with the most confusing shite and rudest words of which you can possibly think. Judicious use of the terms 'fucken' and 'fuck off' are highly recommended.

Chapter *Five*

Neural Transmissions and Bad Behaviour

THERE IS ONE OTHER THING to be considered when selecting your saviour. You may want to think about going to an actual medical shrink for the drugs. Because some of us have a teensy little habit of self-medicating, don't we? It is not advisable to take a beer bong on top of an E on top of whatever the health food shop claims will fix depression this week on top of homoeopathic melotonin and some of your mum's Serapax. And you know, you fucking lot who gobble that St John's wort (for the uninitiated, currently a wildly popular and unscheduled 'herbal' prophylactic against depression) like it is going out of style, maybe you should TALK to somebody about it. ANY drug or vitamin or bloody floral root that has an effect on your mood should be considered seriously. Do not take things willy-nilly! Believe me, I totally and intimately know the desire to shove things in your mouth, in your arse, up your arm or in your schnozz! The fact is, nine times out of ten, drugs don't bloody work. If you can't stay off stimulants or downers, at least tell your shrink exactly how you are taking a claw hammer and a three-inch drill bit to your poor synapses. Give him or her the opportunity of prescribing for you more precisely. Just say no. Or at least, just say Not Until Next Tuesday. And call me nanna, but I think that pot is shite. It is a fucking psychedelic. Is so. And one or two of the people I ADORE are going to hate me for imparting my pot hatred. But, hello, it makes you PARANOID. And causes Cadbury's Milk Tray dependency. Do not skin up quite so often. One has done one's share of jazz cigarette puffing. One knows what one is on about. And don't give me that bovine 'it is relaxing and people have been doing it for thousands of years and it is NATURAL' shite either. So is having sex with farmyard animals. Doesn't make it good for your mental health. I have no respect for this narcotic. I know it makes wanking a load more fun, but just stop it. Or smoke a bit less.

On the other hand there are also those of you who refuse to take anything at all. Not even something that has been heartily recommended by an excellent shrink. Please don't give me that I'm Too Strong And Capable And Self-Reliant for drugs, I am *Über* Man or Woman crap either. If you're that damn butch, then why are you crying like an abandoned baby, carving inverted pentagrams into your forearms and listening to Joy Division naked and alone and weeping in the dark? I don't mean to be a narcotic-loving piglet, but sometimes this stuff can help. I can say with absolute certainty that Cipramil has offered me some relief. And Serzone too. And that Xanax stopped me from doing some pretty stupid things. Of course, I'm a little humiliated about my susceptibility to serotonin and her good friend dopamine. I would have liked to have wrestled all Hemingwayesque with the slippery ichthyoid of my sadness. I would have adored to emerge all Nietzschean from my ordeal, smug in the knowledge that I had overcome without drugs. (If you think about it, neither Ernest nor Fred were very happy blokes. Actually, if Selective Serotonin Reuptake Inhibitors had been around, maybe they'd have had a fighting chance. And maybe Ernest wouldn't have written those awful novels. Which would have been good, I reckon. I bloody hate Hemingway.)

It is a healthy impulse to be suspicious of drugs. Especially of the soporific-type pills like Vals, Moggies, Normies, Xanax, Serapax and the whole nine yards. My personal passion for a good solid sleeping draught has managed to ruin many promising days. Drugs can suck. And, who knows, Cipramil and Serzone have only recently been approved, so maybe I'll grow a third arm or a penis or die of pancreatic cancer. But who gives a shit really? The fact is, the antidepressant and antianxiety medication helped me stay away from the knife drawer. And I do think that it would be nice if you could keep your distance from pointy objects too. So maybe you should consider seeing a therapist who is qualified to use a prescription pad.

I don't want to come over like one of those SSRI champion dullards, but Prozac and her friends can really work. And RIMAs too, and whatever else. One of the reasons Prozac accrued such a wild reputation is that it did actually appear to transform people's personalities. I personally don't suspect that Cipramil or Serzone transmutated my 'essence' (whatever that fucking is) but they did help to get my serotonin back up to something like the median level for fifty-five kilograms of sad female flesh. So, to all appearances, I had been fed a Wonder Drug that took me from egregious yabbering nincompoop to reasonable human in a matter of six weeks. And I say thank fuck for fluoxotine, or whatever it is that resides in those humble little white tablets. As long as my neural transmitters are behaving somewhere between forlorn and content, I'm happy. It's better than dealing with a scale that begins with misery and ends with suicide attempts.

Look, I should be a teensy bit more honest with you. Cipramil DID make me a bit zombielike. I found it to be a despotic, odd and meandering pitch shifter. And it conferred upon me the worst dizzy spells. And I went off it for a while, and went back on it again, and the second time around I got SO depressed. And Serzone seemed okay, although it made me lose about five kilograms very quickly and enhanced my desire to smoke cigarettes. If you are a skinny type, be careful with antidepressants. I lost like fifteen kilograms over twelve months. And I am still losing weight, although I have ditched the drugs. And I have no appetite. And although one would not KNOW and one has merely heard stories, Serzone was, for me, pretty much like taking an E for the first few days. Oh shite. Now you drug-pigs and anorexics are going to go out and find some. However, I do not like E and I despise euphoria and imagine, even as I experience it, that it is bad for my health. Also, Serzone made me like techno a lot. Further, I kept acquiring burdensome crushes on people. Which is just not like me! Seriously.

But if you feel it is correct, give the chemicals a go. Go on! You've been at your synapses with a sledgehammer for months now. A few little pills can't hurt you that much. As for the long-term effects? Well, we don't know yet, do we? But I'd rather have twenty happy years on the planet than a miserable and further fifty. Oh dear, a little bleak, no? You know what I mean, though.

Much has been written, apparently, about the tyranny of Prozac and her friends. I haven't read any of these texts. Too scared! I have heard, however, that SSRIs are (a) definitely less effective in ablating depression the second time round, and (b) potentially depressive themselves when a second course is attempted. SSRIs are, it must be said, tempestuous and a little like antibiotics in that they can actually forge purported side effects that are more problematic than the object of their destruction: the disease itself. (NB: To sate any curiosity you might have, go to a search engine with several fields such as hotbot or lycos and choose the 'title' option and type in the name of your drug. You will, of course, end up in the officially ratified sites. But the user-generated message boards can provide legitimate help in chronicling what to expect on a particular medication.)

I have volitionally avoided works that gesticulate toward the long-term effects of SSRI. My account here, as always, has its foundation in naught but experience. It has been some time since I discarded the repeat prescription. Actually it's getting on to an entire pure year! Occasionally, I encounter strange phrenic eruptions that have much, I feel sure, to do with chemical memory. Sort of like flashbacks but without people turning into goats.

Further, I (infrequently) confront an uncomfortable wave of dizzy passivity, cannot maintain the rage in situations where I require it! I have come over all benign and heifer-like in recent months and I attribute this to SSRI. It was worse when I was actually withdrawing from the chemical. Half-woman, half-livestock.

My metabolism, these days, is erratic. I take weight off with alacrity, but also pile it on, on occasion. SSRIs, particularly just when I ceased imbibing them, put me off my food. I felt ill and turned into a size six, or something equally implausible, and I really needed to eat regularly. I have, I think, been left with a dim trace of an eating disorder.

Essentially, prepare to apprehend antidepressants as duplicitous poison, once you're off them. Oh, and another thing, don't come off antidepressants suddenly and don't do it without medical supervision. Come off them gradually and sensibly.

But while you're on them, it's important not to hate yourself for being reliant on 'crutches'. You're sick, you are (please) getting the best available assistance and, I hope, you are asking sensible questions and getting your shrink or pharmacist to draw little pictures of a neural cleft for you. This, I think, is the ideal: you are thoroughly involved in, but not the sole architect for, your recovery. And really, it's normal to chastise yourself for seeming too dependent. Only the other week, I was drifting along my high street chiding myself for taking drugs. I was all 'I'm a junkie. I'm addicted!'. What a waste of my time. You need help. Receive it.

Just remember: you take enough of anything and it is gonna ruin you, yes? Please use your noggin. I do NOT recommend the abuse or casual apprehension of Prozac or any other bloody chemical, okay?

However, many of us do succumb to:

BAD BEHAVIOUR

I must concede. I do rather like benzos. Quite a lot. Like so many anxious depressives, for me sleep or semiconsciousness is heaven. Delightful and rarely visited. Gorgeous. Respite. Fluffy. Rosaceous. Perfect. The Only Thing. Aaah.

Despite my preference for these pills and my indefatigable passion for blandness, I was in the care of a shrink who did not over prescribe. One who diligently warned of the dangers. So I didn't really get into them. I was made way too cognisant of the steps to getting better. Too conscious of an appropriate trajectory toward peace. Too sick of being fucking sick. So I abstained, more or less. Well, sort of. But Goddess knows, I may not have. Some days I just really wanted to take a shitload of smack. Fortunately, I'm such a relative drug naif that I was too troubled and paranoid and agoraphobic and fractured to get into the entire wearing worried black clothes and waiting at the pub trip. But I wanted to blot it all out. And I developed an ENORMOUS jealousy of junkies. I harboured so much resentment. I thought: there they are with their subculture and their Nick Cave and their icons and their emergency relief programs and their HIV prevention buses where they can all summit and whoop it up and have a good old scaggy time. And they're thin. And people in hospitals know what to do for them.

I thought: if only I could develop a weighty addiction too, then maybe my crisis would be so damn obvious that somebody would do something for me also.

I think a lot of depressives and general free-floating fruitbats feel like this. First we feel like we should acquire some tenable, solid and altogether less nebulous ailment so that someone will look after us. Second, drugs can be really bloody handy in making you feel better. Anyway, some of us end up taking them, don't we? Not necessarily smack. As every young modern knows, heroin is not the only dark delight available to us. Bloody codeine tablets or cough medicine or flat lager will do at a pinch.

I really do think that drug dependency emerges from depression. Even if the depression is latent and unacknowledged. Of course there are probably one or two people who are simply content yet greedy truffle pigs who will snort, spike or swallow whatever happens to be going about at that juncture. Don't reckon there's many of them but.

Whatever the bloody case, I don't know of too many anxious trifles and depressed fancies who have not indulged in one form of compulsive behaviour or another. So rather silly of me of course to envy addicts when they are really just like me with a whole lot more work to do and infinitely more nuisance in their poor fraught lives. So I'm dreadfully contrite for looking longingly at the needle-exchange bus. I really am.

Whether you're a long-term habitué of Bad Behaviour, or you've just come to it recently, do please be careful. As I have admonished previously, you with your desultory thought patterns and challenged bodies and hissy fits and what not need all the peace and calm you can get. Drugs or compulsive behaviours really don't provide this at all. Duh, Miss Helen.

I am reluctant to offer any specific advice re compulsive behaviour or substance abuse as I just don't feel qualified. Besides which, there's a whole truckload of other books and organisations that concern themselves ably with these topics.

And I do not wish to conjecture (although many would) that Bad Behaviour (sinking piss, taking smack, gambling, anorexia etc) is ALWAYS the corollary of depression and anxiety. Although, often-times—I think we will be in accord here—it is. Given this premise, that Bad Behaviour may be a symptom of anxiety and depression, then I proffer a few feeble words.

In Behaving Badly, you are simply making the journey toward recovery, or personally tailored sanity, more protracted. You are obfuscating. Giving yourself a harder time than is necessary. Constructing obstructions. Duh. The other thing you are possibly doing, as indicated previously in my smack fragment, is attempting to get better in an erroneous fashion. That is, if you allow your entire mode of production, life etc, to be geared toward substance abuse, vomiting, self-flagellation, glory-hole visits and what not, then you might be attempting to give yourself something to 'fix'. Anxiety and depression, of course, are somewhat nebulous by nature. Sinking a load of piss isn't. There is evidence of your piss-artistry. Empty bottles, vomit, bad breath, etc. And such obvious, relatively structured distemper implies the possibility of cure more potently than unadorned anxiety and depression. Further, as mentioned, there appears to be more professional assistance available for lushes than to depressives and anxious bunnies.

Overtly, if and when you do actually stem the Bad Behaviour, you are going to be left with the anxiety and depression in any case. So stop it now. I can't tell you how to. I haven't completely stopped myself. Nicotine, alcohol, caffeine, the occasional benzo and a whole series of embarrassing compulsive disorders that I do not wish to chronicle still inform me.

I can say, though, if you try to stop Behaving Badly and only manage it for a week or so, don't give yourself too much of a hard time. You have not failed too miserably. Just give it another Aussie go. You have simply stumbled.

Of course, if you are doing harm to your body (losing stupid weight, gaining stupid weight, acquiring speed psychosis, coughing up oysters, cutting yourself) or pissing off those you love by stealing their stereos WORK ON IT HARD. And, really, it might be a good idea to chastise yourself to the point where you no longer do these unethical, harmful things. And it is best to avoid getting arrested, of course. (I was held for about six hours in a police station one time and did not find the interview process, the fingerprinting or the lock up bit very soothing at all. Good situation to avoid.)

In short, stop it. Please. Or at least strive to slow down. Look at your compulsion head on. Try to contain or mutate it.

Chapter *Six*

Techniques for Surviving Depression

I REPEATEDLY PRONOUNCED THROUGHOUT the course of my (partial) recovery a self-devised dictum: anxiety is explosive; depression is implosive. Anxiety is where you flood uncontrollably into the world. Depression is when the world comes seeping in on you. Not very profound, I know. But when you're sick, kids, simplicity can be key. (Did Miss Needless Complexity just say that?)

My depression was, and remains, dank, oppressive and vile. Although it has never really felt, in the manner of anxiety, like a Tormentor. Anxiety, as we will discuss in the appropriate chapter (jeez I love myself when I sound that darn organised! WEE HEE), can be turned into a monster with relative ease. You can personify it, reify it and give it a name. All the self-help books will tell you this. Cajole your anxiety. Offer it blandishments and entreaties to do its worst. Think of it as a parasite. Some folks I have spoken with imagine their anxiety to be something like an annoying sibling who simply tags along. If you relax and eventually just acknowledge its separate presence, it may become less horrific in time. Depression, although intimately linked, in my experience, to anxiety, is a different beast altogether.

Recovery from anxiety requires that you relocate and reassemble all the messy pieces of your 'self' until existence becomes tenable. It is as though you have erupted. Given this emotional template, which many people I know have experienced, reconstruction is always a vague possibility. Recovering from anxiety is like putting together a puzzle. Annoying, but tenable. Anxiety, in short, is more manageable than depression. Okey-doke, you muse in more lucid moments, there's a bit of me over there by the night stand and if I can just summon up the energy, I can whack it back where it belongs, or maybe find an intriguing new place to keep it. Depression isn't so knowable.

Anxiety appears to emanate from within. Depression, by contrast, is like an external force. The 'fact' of your personhood becomes so very very small in relation to its presence. It doesn't so much devour you as crush you to the point of total servitude. On bad days it just seems so much easier to yield to its simple demands. Which, in my case, were mostly along the lines of: lie in bed and don't get up for a couple of years. And occasionally I would consider suicide to be the only solution to my depressive bouts. Well, actually, NOT occasionally. Most of the time. Tsk tsk. We have to banish such thoughts. Honestly. Never top yourself. It has a tendency to really piss your friends off. And really, some dickhead will eulogise you all wrong at the funeral. Suicide is just silly and NOT an option.

WHAT DO I DO WHEN DEPRESSION STARTS FEELING LIKE THE TRUTH?

A horrible thing about depression, I have noticed, is that I can fool myself, when profoundly down, into thinking I have had an epiphany. You know, a really complex, multilayered holy experience. How? In what mode? Well that takes a little explaining. Often depression cruelly follows a serious bout of acute anxiety disorder. It did with me anyway. You go about feeling shattered and devoid of any sensible reactions to anything for a couple of months and then BAM one day you wake up keenly aware of everything. In my case, I had the disorder called hypervigilance immediately prior to my serious depression. That is, I went from not hearing or seeing or tasting or feeling much at all, except an internally manufactured pain, to screeching every time one of my sensory receptors was challenged. Cats, buses, shop assistants or whatever would make me start. This hypervigilance heralded the start of my depression.

Everything left its imprint on me. I felt like a big wet fucking human sand box. Gradually the world grew larger and I became microscopic and unthinkably weak. And at some point, the faux epiphany happened. Let me explain a little better . . .

I felt, in my infinite smallness, as though I had some kind of knowledge or hitherto unexplored connection to 'reality' or to the nature of things. Although fucking miserable and awash with noisome self-loathing, I almost felt privileged at times to be visited by this depression. I felt, after so many months of not reacting to anything at all, save my own heart palpitations and hyperventilation and whatnot, that something important was revealing itself to me. Finally, I mused, I was connecting with the world. Pretty weird if I think about it now because in fact I had never been so cut off and idiotic and alone in my life before! I had never been so divorced from that thing we collectively choose to call reality. Nonetheless, I started having these I AM THE TRUTH suspicions. You know, just between us, I even (casually, sardonically) considered going to church a number of times. Which is a pretty big deal for someone who professed utter atheism in kindergarten. One has never prayed, not even during arrant aero-turbulence over the north pole. Not even when I was eighteen and thick and underpoliticised and suddenly in the company of a Turkish soldier in Erzurum who was brandishing his gun and gesturing toward my chest with it and telling me not to talk to Kurds (even though I wasn't at all sure that that was (a) what I had done and (b) why that should be a fucking problem in any case). Never talked to God. Never felt a trace of it. So it was rather unprecedented that I should begin having religious feelings, you know? I guess I assumed I would amaze the assembled parishioners with my Messianic, red-alert-line-to-God type ambience.

I have spoken to so many people during and after their depression who report having harboured similar Godlike notions. Some of us depressives fuddle about feeling all metaphysical and honest. We know the foundation, with our great taproot. We have been there! As poor old (dead) Sylvia said. We think we are so very wise. The essential thing to remember is that, actually, we are all just having a great big sad old hissy fit and there's actually nothing of interest down there at the bottom.

Honestly, there's not! When you are so very depressed, it is, from one standpoint, a method of self-preservation to think that you know the world as it 'really is'. At the very least you feel mildly functional being the bearer of deepest epistemic sincerity. You are somewhat soothed by the suspicion that you, you and precious only you can logically unpeel the secrets to existence. It is comforting to think that this behemoth, depression, has come to bestow You Special You with essential knowledge. From what I can gather, however, such musings can easily end in suicide. And boredom. And abject stupidity. And religion, eek.

Keep telling yourself that depression is NOT an educative state! You are only going to learn useless shit, like how long you can go without using the bog or having a wash or eating. Or how many superfluous hairs you have on your right nipple. Or exactly how many red jelly cups you can devour in a single bleak afternoon. Or how few REAL friends you truly have. Or how much your cat genuinely despises you. Or how many futile units you completed at uni. Or how sour your armpits genuinely can become. Or what happens when you abandon your beauty regimen so thoroughly. Or how few relatives seem to give a toss about your thorough unmitigated breakdown. Or how your seven times table seems to elude you. Or the length of days.

DEPRESSION DOES NOT TEACH YOU ANYTHING. It may turn you, ultimately, into a person more tolerant of others' foibles. You might get a few half-decent poems out of it. But please don't be proud of your depression. Don't buy that There's-A-Fine-Line-Between-Genius-And-Insanity shit. You learn nothing from depression. Except how to hate yourself with TOTAL efficacy and minimum effort. By contrast, what you learn from your recovery could fill an entire zip drive with text, I'm sure! Try to listen to yourself when you are depressed. All you come out with is, why should I fucking bother? The world is ugly. My penis is a sad protuberance. My womb is poison. And other ephemeral aphorisms. And then, for a contrast, try to record your feelings as you climb out of the hole. Orotundity and wisdom are byproducts of mental health. All depression does is turn you into a blithering sick boring painful futile noisome fuckstick. (It's okay to be a blithering sick boring painful futile noisome fuckstick for a while. Hell, many people earn good money from it. I occasionally work in the electronic media, an industry replete with well-paid fucksticks. Just accept your temporary idiocy. Understand that others will find you tedious for a time—who cares?—and believe that you will get better. And, matey boy, when you do get well, you can begin to be endlessly fascinating again. It is QUITE acceptable to be a nong for a while. Just remember that you are, in fact, a total nong when depressed.)

Depression is not a protective membrane! It's an annoying disease. It's like asthma or something. Dermatitis. I don't know, use your imagination! It's an allergy. That's what it is. An unpleasant and temporary and reducible reaction to, say, oxygen! And don't give me that 'as if' look! I know you, matey boy and matey girl. We are more similar than you might suspect. If you can develop a phobia about soap or birds or the wind, as many of you may have, you can certainly fool yourself into thinking that depression is merely the consequence of an allergy. DEPRESSION IS AN ALLERGY THAT CAN BE MANAGED. I said that to myself. And believe it or not, it worked. Well, eventually. I went to the doctor a lot and took prescribed drugs too. (Which, as noted in the previous chapter, I reckon might have buggered my body a bit.) However, the uncomplicated acknowledgment of being actually SICK is a major step toward better health. And, importantly, the authentic realisation that depression is just a load of useless shit is going to help you so very much. Repeat after me.

Depression teaches me nothing. Except how unctuous and unwashed I can become. Recovery will teach me everything. The better I get, the smarter I will become. Okay?

WHAT DO I DO WHEN I FEEL MY DEPRESSION IS THE SOURCE OF ALL MY ENERGY AND WORTH?

Letting go of depression, which is an ongoing process for me, is problematic in manifold ways. Possibly depression had been a latent force for a great part of my life. As such, I had become completely immune to any perspective contrary to the depressive one. As with many depressives I have spoken to, phrenic qualities such as intelligence, a highly developed critical faculty and cynicism were vital to my world view and sense of 'self'. I could not, for example, ever be happy for someone I liked when they achieved success. It was always like 'Yeah, well she might have a new job as editor, but it's a shit magazine' or 'That guy's band sucks because they all have body piercings, they're so five minutes ago'. Or whatever. Lots of mean, classic Glass Half Empty stuff. If, I reasoned, I did not evince these nasty opinions, then I was obviously a lame dickhead. Most of the time I was not even aware that I was being cynical. I just assumed that I was being honest.

Further, I reasoned, if I did not maintain such almighty High Standards, then my own creative output would suffer. If I succumbed to the appallingly impoverished demands of a crap world, then I too would be crap. Now, this spurious depressive logic can work for any endeavour. You don't have to be a wanky media and performance type like me to suffer such delusions. You can be a carpenter, a parent or a philatelist. You can become depressed and fixated on the way you paint your nails for god's sake! And you can get punitive and nasty about other people just as easily.

It occurred to me recently that cynicism is simply a byproduct of depression. You may note when you're getting well that the world tastes and feels different to you. You may find the most banal things fascinating. I did, and it kind of worried me at first. I kept saying to my shrink, 'I feel like I'm five. The colour pink intrigues me and I'm amazed that they can put those ships in bottles!' I thought I was really going mad when simple things began to lure my attention. He told me I was getting well. Experiencing an uncluttered and relatively content mode of perception for the first time! Currently I'm still noticing that the oddest things reveal themselves to me in new ways. That I might actually be happy for my friend because she got a new television pilot! That my mate's film might have been poorly edited, but it did have a great fractious antinarrative. It is actually cool to feel this way. It is liberating.

And the other thing, once you start to drop the hate, you become less intropunitive. I was convinced that I would not be able to write when my depression left me. I thought that it was a rich vein of inspiration. However, every day my writing becomes more technically adept and, another happy corollary, more widely published. You have to stop fretting that depression informs your working, creative self. Your chosen professional ability, in many cases, is one of the first things to return during recovery. Sure, it may have totally departed for a while. However, rest assured (as much as a depressive can either rest or, for that matter, be assured!) that new and/or improved skills will return, in time, with a vengeance. When my SSRI and therapy kicked in and I ACTUALLY STOPPED crying, I became almost unreasonably productive. And the verve I so obviously displayed for my work was apparent to my various employers. For me, there was (and remains) a lot of stuff to fix in my head after the desire to be productive returned. And maybe I worked so hard writing and performing and doing television pilots in order to divert my attention from the relationships I'd ruined. But hell, I say if it feels a little bit good and it gives you pleasure and gets you one or two elephant stamps, fucking consolidate! Affirm the unusual energy that follows a serious depression. Work, try to get reasonable sleep and eat your dinner, and just enjoy the accolades if they occur.

If you're down a bit deep down right now, please please please try to believe that your enthusiasm and abilities will return in truckloads. That's not a vacuous promise designed to keep you on Prozac and away from the knife drawer. You will, I promise, become more adept at thinking, doing and articulating than you ever have been in your life. It's a strange little bonus, this one. Your intellect will return. And be better and unfettered by the nasty misery beast. Lots of shit disappeared for me when I was getting well. I stopped procrastinating, started getting to appointments on time and started writing at double speed. And another odd thing. My relationship to fear altered. When you have planned your own death and/or feared it, everything else seems so innocent by contrast. If you have known what it is like to quake uncontrollably in the knowledge that you will surely die soon, then things like job interviews sort of become small potatoes.

Depression and fear may be viewed, in time, as useful tools. As annoying diseases that, bizarrely enough, produce lifelong benefits. Recovery really optimises your brain. It's just true, okay? You won't get stupid by being happy. You won't become useless by letting go of your depressive illness.

WHAT DO I DO WHEN I HATE MYSELF RATHER A LOT?

There are those days when you feel so resolutely down that getting up is not even a dim fucking possibility. What can you do to combat that sort of depression where you just want to go to sleep for a really really long time? Or you just want to evaporate? I want to talk more specifically about suicidal thoughts later, in the chapter 'First Aid', okay?

So, how do we deal with that level of depression which immediately precedes fantasies of topping ourselves? Personally, I attempt one of two methods. The first works (sometimes wanly!) for the serious twenty-kilos-of-metal-just-fell-on-my-head kind of depression.

Method Number One: I just let it get really bad. I make detailed lists of how much I loathe myself. I chronicle all the tasks I am no longer able to competently complete. I review all the people I have ever weirded out. I commemorate all my crimes against humanity. And I do this until it gets ridiculous. Until even I can say, at my nadir, 'Well that's dumb!' I get to the point where I criticise my teeth, my giggle, my shoes and my breath. I arrive at a place so absurd I find even my method of digesting food repulsive. I recall that I no longer sit on the toilet in an acceptable mode. I commence an obtuse hatred of my ear lobes. I become humiliated by EVERYTHING! By making the asinine conceptual leaps afforded by depression, I hold myself responsible as the progenitor of patriarchy, racism and feeble fast-food chains. I get so down and so stupid on myself that even I have to laugh. I let the wave consume me. Hell, it's going to anyway. I am dumped in my own ludicrous, self-hating frothy excess. I paddle in the waste of my own oozing paranoia. I hate myself so thoroughly that there's nowhere left to go but the comic shore! Let it all get to the point where even you have to laugh. I know a lot of folks think he's cheesy, but Milan Kundera has much to say about this in *The Book of Laughter and Forgetting*. (Hey, fuck you if you think he's trite. Remember, we are supposed to relinquish our cynicism and parlous fucking judgment. If I want to admit that I like soppy old Milan, then bugger you, matey!) As an expatriate Czech, Kundera deals with the pain felt by his countryfolk at the hands of communism done in the Joe Stalin style. Now I don't want to come over all hippy and metaphorically fascistic and say that everything is analogous to depression. However, some parallels may be drawn between depressive whackos like us and disenfranchised citizens beaten into submission by a totalitarian regime that surpasses logic. Okay? Yes then, I'll shut up about that now. Whatever the case, and regardless of my distinctly depressed need to apologise and rationalise everything, Kundera says some cool things about the ameliorative power of laughter. Oh, just read the book, would you? Who am I anyway? Carl Fucking Jung? I don't think so. I'm just some chick.

Method Number Two: I note how easily I am affected by things. I reason, 'Well, if an uncomfortable bus trip can make me puce with self-flagellating rage, then a nice milkshake might make me obscenely happy. Let's take this suggestibility for a walk.' Sadly, this method of managing depression only works if you know where to get a flawless milkshake. There's other shit to do of course. A lot of people I know recommend buying an animal, though I reckon that the purchase of a puppy is a tall order for somebody who can barely look after themselves. However, if you're a real quadruped-identified person, go for it. Getting an animal on loan is also quite an idea. I 'borrowed' the neighbour's cat and his sweet little mews actually motivated me to go to the supermarket to buy tinned fish. I couldn't have been bothered previously to go and get food for myself. A fat black pussycat got me back on to the high street. Also, I go home to my parents a lot to visit Tessie Puppy. She is a Cavalier King Charles spaniel and so endlessly comic and dear. When she needs a walk, I simply have to take her. Otherwise she is likely to defecate on my person or chew upon my fake Gucci kitten heels.

Gardening may help. Having rather black thumbs, however, I do note that this can be a very disheartening exercise if your plants fuck up. Also, you have to wait months to see results. Maybe a little basil in a pot. And don't take its seasonal decline personally!

Further, I have, as you know, dabbled in Wiccan magick. Let me hasten to add here that I am a polynontheist and I don't believe in anything. I did find, however, that casting little protection spells for myself helped me along. We beings tend to ritualise just about all major events in our lives. We mark birth, death, love, infidelity and puberty with formal or semiformal rites. Believe me, forlorn pusscats, your depression is one of the most important, incendiary and formative events of your life. Learn how to acknowledge it. Find ways in which to articulate your recovery. My best friend Fiona told me to put nine rusty nails under my door to keep the bad things away. Now, as aforementioned, I am simply not the type to bumble about worshipping Gaia or contriving bas-relief depictions of Celtic burial mounds or menstruating on the shrubbery 'neath the new moon. There ain't no goddess in my realm! But the very act of doing something devised entirely for myself lightened my mood. The nails are still under my mat, bidding an insistent, insouciant and symbolic Fuck Off to all who wish me harm. So magick might work.

Many stern rectums will probably be admonishing you for your lethargy and prescribing all manner of fitness schemes. Especially bloody yoga. Yoga, exercise and shit like that only really works if you've got to the point of leaving the house and are actively seeking respite. Don't even attempt any of this guff unless you're feeling strong-ish. Months of failing the lotus position can really rip your already frayed bib. Please be wary of yoga. I do concede that this exercise may, in time, prove soothing and healthful and such. However, since bloody Madonna started banging on about it, everybody and her dog is going on with 'Oh my gosh, you really have to try some yoga! It really CENTRES you.' To which I generally reply, 'Centre is not a fucking verb in my universe, thanks.' Frankly, you need an iron will, a relatively steady body and untold patience for something as extreme as yoga.

Beware of any hobby or assistance that may prove too complex or demanding. For some odd reason, the depressed and anxious will generally attempt the impossible, implausible and unpleasant exactly when they shouldn't! Refuse the tyranny of fucking stupid masochistic bullshit. If you feel like slithering into a gym, only do a little weight work and some minor fat burn or cardio if you must, and then just go straight for the massage, for heaven's sake! Have a bloody facial instead of an intensive (and absurd) inner woman weekend workshop. Your resolve to do just about anything is weakened. And of course your self-esteem is low and susceptibility to personal failure damnably high! So don't attempt nonsensical things. Strive for pleasure and relative passivity in your trajectory toward 'self-improvement'. Don't be a dick. Don't do abseiling or mountain climbing or anything Pepsi Max or fallaciously 'spiritual'. Don't strive to swim dickety million kilometres in an afternoon and don't let expensive weirdos do painful things to your chakras. Don't endeavour to learn the Windows NT operating system in fifteen minutes. Don't chastise yourself for never having acquired advanced VCR recording skills. Don't start a course in hermeneutics. Don't toil away at anything horrible and parlous if you are guided by the assumption that you require a challenge. You do not need another fucking challenge. You've got one, okay? You have to get better. That is in itself a monu-fucking-mental challenge.

If you try to attain some improbable skill in a depressed state, the chances are good DUH that you will simply fuck up. Don't set yourself up for disaster. Aim toward tenable goals. Like having afternoon tea without crying into your point sandwich, for example. I know it sounds very Nanna to cajole 'You look tired. Here, have some passionfruit sponge', but sometimes a slice of delightful sponge cake and a good lie-down can work wonders.

Oh, and humiliating admission time. I have myself recently started attending afternoon tea. Generally this is quite affordable and can be secured in lavish five star surrounds for well under twenty dollars. It is very soothing.

Avoid sad things if at all possible. Turn off the television when those mawkish telephone company ads appear. Don't, as I did, listen to Temple of the Dog, followed by Neil Young's *Harvest* and compound the whole sad polymisanthropic opus with Hole's saddest songs. Choose WHAM!'s greatest hits or a pre-acid Beatles album. Even if it embarrasses the bejesus out of you. Don't read Emily Dickinson, Sylvia Plath, Rimbaud or anybody miserable. Choose *Romy And Michele's High School Reunion*, *Clueless* or *Hollywood Hot Tubs 4* at the video store instead of Ingmar Bergman, for heaven's sake! Oh, and avoid wearing black if you can. I dyed every item of my clothing jet! What a sad, pubescent, torpid, twee waste of a girl am I?

So, don't imagine that you can learn anything. Depression makes you stupid, mute and languid. Recovery helps you emerge as brilliant, garrulous and ebullient.

Chapter *Seven*

Living with Anxiety

R OTTEN CHAPTER TITLE, ISN'T IT? After intensive workshopping and advice from my shrink (I jest, of course. I do make some relevant decisions without his assistance!) it was all I could come up with. I mean, I'd really like to have a more involute and irreverent attitude to my own fear than this title would suggest. To be candid, however, my anxiety still scares the bejesus out of me from time to time. It'll be a while before I can make stupendous fun of my little turns. So excuse the neomystic I'm OK, You're OK emphasis contained within the above syllables.

As the vast majority of my intimates are nearly as whacked as I am, I knew all about panic attacks when I first had one. I was apprised of the symptoms and, to a limited degree, of strategies to combat them. Many of you, I am shocked and saddened to learn, have not a clue what is happening to you when you first wig out. To be candid, that would have scared the shit out of me! So, for those of you who suspect that all is not right in the realm of your bod and shattered psyche, I'd better list the garden-variety panic attack symptoms. You MUST be apprised of the fact and potency of your anxiety before you begin to thwart it. So here goes . . .

AM I HAVING AN ANXIETY ATTACK?

If your particular brand of psychotic idiocy is not documented here, don't worry. The chances are great that somebody else has beaten you to the pages of *Psychology Today*. Anxiety manifests in countless forms. Here are a few of them.

Tunnel vision is a personal favourite. At the height of my anxiety my senses shut down. First it was the eyes, then everything sounded like I was underwater and pretty soon touch was irksome, taste was nonexistent and smell had gone on a short vacation. Others report enhanced rather than dulled sensitivity, which manifests as the phenomenon known to shrinkos as **hypervigilance**. (I like that phrase, personally, it made me feel special! Sounds like something Jean Baudrillard would write about.) You know that one. The tiniest sound can make you start. Music is deafening. The sun is impossible. Taste is repugnant. Mildly offensive smells work your gut into a frenzy. Everything appears to have hideously sharp edges. Your pillow slip threatens to turn your face into shreds. All that gear. A friend of mine actually reported a sort of minor **synaesthesia**. That's when you think you can smell colour, savour sound, feel visible objects without touching them, et cetera. Cross-wired senses, essentially. I also became a temporary synaesthete. (Which was pretty rotten, I must say. I have always found that my favourite recordings have great power to soothe me. Sadly for poor old disenfranchised me, *Physical Graffiti* and *Sticky Fingers* and *Horses* caused my vision to blur and my stomach to rebel as though it had imbibed something poisonous. I couldn't return to my preferred music for an age for fear it would revivify this multisensory disorder.) In any case, there's a pretty good chance that something bizarre will happen to your hitherto functional senses. You may, as I did, go to the doctor complaining of impaired vision and mitigated hearing. If they are a half-decent GP, they'll send you to a head-doctor post-haste! There's a good chance you'll find sex, eating and sleep physically repulsive. Without wishing to gross you out thoroughly, you might find defecation and urination similarly problematic. Any practice that is primal, essential and fundamental to your vision of basic subjecthood may be improperly touched by your anxiety. SO MANY THINGS will go wrong with you. I'm so very sorry.

Hyperventilation is very common. This may manifest in an obvious mode and you could find yourself panting, slavering and puffing like a terribly confused basset hound on Ritalin. Or you may not even notice you're doing it. Dizziness and a tingling in your extremities are apparently indications that you're not breathing properly. If your limbs are going to sleep too easily and your mouth feels like it has been recently smothered in fizzy sherbet, there's a good chance that you are hyperventilating. I'll get to breathing exercises later.

Palpitations are widely reported, as are **headaches,** a desire to get the fuck out of wherever you are and solid intimations of **dread.** **Crying,** wailing, **forgetfulness** and the apocryphal gnashing of teeth are also standard fare. Re forgetfulness. One can almost enter a fugue state. I recall one afternoon having no fucking clue where I was. Actually I was just outside the New South Wales Art Gallery where I'd been dickety million times before. I had to call a friend from a phone box—after having dialled dickety million wrong numbers. Why is Telstra Call Connect unavailable from public telephones?—and she asked me to describe the buildings about me. For one wild minute I thought I was outside the New York State Library! (Never been there!) Finally she asked me to read the legend printed on the phone box. You Are Outside The Fucking Art Gallery, Helen, it read. Gosh I was sheepish.

Feelings of **humiliation** were prevalent in my life for a time. I would fitfully recount all the vile, unseemly or dangerous things I had ever enacted and reproduce my shame. This process, in turn, would generally bring on another anxiety attack! And then I'd get sheepish all over again owing to the indiscreet advent of an attack. (We precious, self-obsessed purveyors of personal panic would do well to remember that often our fits of anxiety are invisible to other people. Although an attack may be palpable to you, it may be barely discernible from another's vantage point.) Embarrassment proved such an impediment for me. It was crippling and all-encompassing and deadening. I would often end up, after an Embarrassment Attack, feeling like a burden. When the pangs of humiliation had subsided and I'd managed somehow or other to stop the pathological cringing, I'd feel so damn heavy. I'd feel like a blot. I'd feel as though I was comprised of the densest possible matter and my very presence in the universe turned gravity and all other physical systems awry. I felt responsible. I felt ashamed. You may also experience the most appalling sensation of unworthiness.

Another sensation which often bombarded me was something I can only describe as a **broken head**. Occasionally I was plagued and impeded by the suspicion that my synapses were exploding. I genuinely and regularly perceived a type of phrenic crashing. I was convinced that parts of my brain were dying. I became immobilised by these potent little shocks. And if my brain wasn't in a full self-destructive frenzy, I would often imagine that my poor battered lobes were rolling about yolklike in my feckless eggshell head. I thought my hitherto grandiose bonce would shatter. I felt as though I had lost all ability to think. In retrospect, I concede that these painful indications were necessary and educative. As it happened, my ludicrous cerebrum WAS busy forging new pathways. Thorough metamorphosis WAS occurring. My mental template for manufacturing ideas, my trajectories toward problem solving and my way of coping with emotionally pungent events WERE all transmuting irreversibly! As you travel through the torment of therapy, kids, try to remember that you will enact the changes of a decade, or even a lifetime, in a matter of months.

I also became toweringly **superstitious**. Sometimes I would **hurt myself** as a reminder that I was alive. Vivid, execrable **nightmares**, **paranoia** and a general, all encompassing suspicion of **insecurity** are commonplace. Oh, did I mention **nausea, the trots**, frequent **pissing** and the odd sensation that you no longer fit comfortably inside your body? I think this last conundrum is called **depersonalisation**. Flowery psychiatric shorthand for the worst kind of unsolicited physical departure! This can emerge as a feeling that you are hovering about a centimetre away from yourself. Or it may be more extreme. It could be something along the lines of astral travel. You may feel as though you're looking down on yourself while you're in bed. Try not to fret excessively. You ARE NOT going potty. This is a well documented reaction to anxiety. It's just another execrable corollary of the flight or fight syndrome. Your poor head just wants to get the fuck away from its tormented body. When the fear is too much to bear, your mind pretends it is elsewhere. Nothing much worse than when your brain or your heart or your ears feel like they're in the next room!

Depersonalisation was one of the most problematic symptoms with which I had to grapple. It is SUCH a mind fuck. Further, despite the fact that it was heinously uncomfortable and incomprehensible, I found that I actively resorted to it from time to time. If I was in a challenging, potentially anxiety-producing situation, I would consciously remove myself from it. I usurped my illness to escape from it. Weird, huh? Please be cautious about employing your symptoms to negate the fact of your illness. This process, I guess, deserves another bold type mention in itself. What can we call it? Um. It is a bizarre and negative self-embrace. I don't know how to name it. I am positive, however, that there is an officially ratified psychotherapeutic label for it. Let us just endow it with the title **extreme wobblies** for the moment. Never been much good at neologism myself. As a short aside, many postneurotics have told me that their vocab and general word usage and ability to achieve better confluence in speech and text improved during recovery. Very oddball, no? I tend to think that as one is forced to endure a type of visceral second childhood, the acquisition of language happens all over again. Very oedipal. I would like to discuss recovery as an isomer for childhood in a later chapter, 'Conceptual Potty Training for your Noisome Inner Child', merely because the title amuses me. But I shall not.)

No survey of panic attacks would be complete without a nod to that perennial neurotic's favourite, OH MY GOD I JUST KNOW I'M GOING TO DIE. (Please refer to the section in 'First Aid' on managing this irksome phenomenon.) Or that something has to be replaced, amputated or steam-cleaned. Or that someone or something is going to emerge from your closet and eat/rape/dismember/sauté you. Or that the world has actually inverted. Or everything looks two-dimensional. Or that if you visit a particular building, street, postcode, city or country, your bottom will fall off. Then there are **phobias**. Hmmm, phobias. As mentioned earlier, I actually developed one about a particular brand of soap. Also, one about Libran men (odd, considering I deem astrology to be a load of dolphin detritus), wattle, springtime, the word inchoate, the 412 bus route, Shiseido cosmetics, red meat, Pizza Hut, the Yahoo search engine and mosquitoes. Did I mention English muffins, an entire suburb and newspapers?

Silence Now, Ms Razer, And Let's Chat About Dealing With A Hissy Fit.

HOW DO I DEAL WITH A PANIC ATTACK?

The short answer, of course, is don't. You can't. So don't even try. And if you're reading this chapter at all, you're probably going to have to deal with the vile, punitive, querulous and nasty things for quite a while yet. So just relax (yeah, right!) and let them happen.

You CANNOT overcome fits of anxiety by sheer resilience and force of will. The odd thing about free-floating angst and fear and what have you is their eventual susceptibility to, and death by, their victim's vulnerability. Strangely, the less defensive you are, the quicker you can get better. Strength and power, in their classic incarnations, are not effective when dealing with anxiety. Nakedness, extreme susceptibility and the ability to frequently expose one's poor soft underbelly are qualities you must encourage. Don't battle with your anxiety. Let it win. Let it do its worst. I found that it was only when I had embraced the Gargantuan nature of my weakness that I became dangerous enough to elude these shitty hissy fits. Here I'd like to offer some of the strategies I have developed to deal with my own nebulous terror.

Freeing yourself from anxiety is problematic. Well, duh. It takes a lot of psychotherapeutic unravelment and assiduous homework. There are some tactics, however, to quiet the serotonin-zapping beast in the short-term.

Be a Selfish Piggie. The most fundamental tool in your antianxiety arsenal is selfishness. You simply can't afford to care what other people think. So what if your friends find out you're a fruitbat? If they can't cope with such a pedestrian, manageable occurrence as temporary insanity, then you shouldn't be hanging around with them anyway. They can bugger off. They can go straight to hell. Give them the directions. As for those who read your brief incapacity as a sign of weakness, well they're just unreconstructed fuckwits who didn't deserve you in the first place. Every ounce of energy you have should be geared toward steadying yourself. Try to simply announce that you are ill and hide in the toilet until the demons have departed. BE SELFISH.

You're going to have to change your behaviour. Do nice things for yourself whenever possible. If you can't yet locate or manage to find events and objects that please you, at least try to avoid doing things that displease you. In the early stages of your anxiety disorder, simply avoid people, scenarios and places that make you feel ill. For me this meant not watching the news, putting my head down when I saw the pan-handlers I used to give money to, and totally avoiding the morose poetry of Emily Dickinson. If a certain shopping mall, breed of cat or basic food group gives you the ineffable shits, remove it from your sphere until you are desensitised enough to confront it. AND THAT COULD TAKE YEARS. YEARS, I'M TELLING YOU! YEARS! You don't have the time to worry about global warming, world peace and whether or not your next-door neighbour has started to notice that you never leave the house. Don't do anything to upset yourself. And if, as many Stress Queens are, you happen to be one of those motivated, charitable and feeling types, don't give yourself superfluous grief about not doing anything nice for other people for a while. There are people to perform good works and kindness in your absence. All right? You are not indispensable. The world will continue to revolve without your altruism. Furthermore, you will be much better equipped to restore universal harmony when you have surpassed the urge to vomit, scream and quake for no apparent reason.

Breathe, Honey, Breathe. Apparently, we can ingest way too much oxygen and make ourselves worse, so we need to CO_2 up. I am fond of the antiquated brown paper bag as a remedy. I stick my porcine schnozz into somebody else's lunch, if that's all that's available, and then I take big gulps of my own gaseous waste product.

The other way is to hold your breath for ten seconds. Apparently, I am advised by august health care professionals, this serves to rid a hissy boy or gal of needless oxygen. Then, expectant horde, we begin to ventilate correctly. While it may be somewhat mortifying to acknowledge that you have, in fact, forgotten how to perform something quite so base as breathing, it happens to the most sterling amongst us. You're not still holding your breath, are you? So, exhale. As you do so in a slow, deliberate and terribly adult fashion, count silently to three. One then two . . . then you pause mid exhale for a tic. A tiny interstice, then slowly express that last third of your breath! If you can, do not gulp for air immediately. Perhaps you might like to count to three again. A short respiratory intermission. Now inhale. One. Two. Little lacuna. Tiny gap! You can do it! (eugh . . . did I just inscribe 'you can do it'? Erky. Veering toward chakra territory!). And then. The last lovely esculent third of your breath may be taken as you phrenically intone 'three'. Excellent. Top job. Have a high fat cheese.

There are other techniques you can discuss with your therapist. I did one involving my pressure points, which kind of worked. However, if you're at all anti-mystic like me, you will diligently avoid anything that seems a bit batik, rough-hewn and natural. That bad brown air out, breathe a rainbow, think of a babbling brook, swim with a great corpulent whale shit never did much good for me. And I'm way too hyper to meditate. You need to find a soothing technique that matches your personal style. Your style is the thing that marks your difference from others, as I've said. Remember to sign your specificity, as I have also said, with the correct stolen goods. When your whole notion of self is disintegrating, try to retain some preferences, proclivities, tastes and what have you. Even in times of crisis. Find something that doesn't make you feel sick or thoroughly embarrassed. Find things that readily 'stick' to you, therapeutically speaking. (My friend Poppy should be footnoted for the adhesion analogy. She often tells me, Be velcro, not teflon, woman! You are a nonstick frying pan today!). If you are suffering hyperhumiliation as I did, this quest for things that glue to you may be fatiguing. So you must be vigilant in your project to mine suitable and expedient therapies for future use. And breathe. Breathe. No, not like *that*! Cease gulping. You don't need THAT much oxygen. Stop it!

Anthropomorphise your Anxiety. That is, turn it into a human, if that seems sensible. In the initial stages of my anxiety disorder, I imagined my panic to be administered by some ogrelike parasite. I thought of myself as a host. I gave the thing some discernible shape. I felt more able to corral the bastard this way. You can turn it into a rat or a virus or whatever. It is good on occasion to think of the damage as being done to you by some alien, imported force. Eventually, you're going to have to learn to coexist with your anxiety. However, I don't perceive the temporary personification of the little brat as a problem. Transmute your anxiety into a serpent or a porpoise or a bull terrier. Turn it into a gnome or a noxious gas or a cane toad. Give it a form. Endow it with metaphor. Turn it, essentially, into something capable of discourse. Whatever. An electronic device, an alien, a shoe. I don't mind. Incarnate your anxiety, and thereby incarcerate it to a delimited extent. Breathe proper life into it. Give it a gender, an address and a top one hundred list of all-time favourite songs chronicled by genre if it helps. Just between us, I endowed my anxiety with a white South African accent. Not nice of me, patently, but it did provide assistance! TURN YOUR ANXIETY INTO A THING! I know it sounds ridiculous. But, look, we're fucking mad anyway. A little mental exercise in metamorphosis isn't going to hurt or embarrass us any more than we have been already! Somewhere down the track, you're going to have to make the conceptual leap and embrace your anxiety in its new contained mode. (After many months, it should be noted, I actually made friends with my anxiety monster and recognised it as a legitimate and integral part of the adipose mass known as Helen Razer.) In time, anxiety will change its querulous shape again and become part of you. For the present, however, just think of it as a punk-ass brat giving you the middle finger. That is, if you have nothing better in mind just yet.

Find Humble Sanctuary. Just as there are locations, moments or people you despise, find things you sort of like. At the very zenith of anxiety, you are probably feeling ambivalent about nearly everything. If you can manage it, however, find a Safe Place or a Comfy Thing. This should be somewhere you have experienced only relatively minor anxious discomfort or some object with which you have shared no problematic history. (Fat Fucking Chance, I hear you implore. Fair cop.) Spend some cash on yourself, if means allow. I found it useful to procure objects that were not yet 'tainted' by my anxiety. Really dumb stuff, if I think about it now. But I sort of instinctively forced myself to purchase brands of food and washing powder I had not previously tried. It's really incredible how we nutbars can imbue even the most insipid and seemingly harmless objects and situations and ENTIRE COUNTRIES with towering semiotic powers. Try to find things and locales that signify NOTHING. Or things that at least shudder with semiotic ambivalence and possibilities. Sometimes we need to surround ourselves with 'immaculate' objects. The simple act of taking a different bus, driving somewhere by a new and circuitous route or showering with a hitherto untested bath gel have the power to transform your mood. Choose to bugger around with your frame of semiotic resonance.

This is not as batty as it sounds. If a shopping trip to Coles can put you in hospital, why then should it not be possible for Woolworths or Safeway to provide deliverance? And remember, although it may not seem like it, you're changing with alacrity. You need to develop a new and profoundly personal symbolic order. You need to invent new meanings for yourself. You need to find things that are free from painful anxious residue. You're a terribly suggestible person in your state. So synthesise new narratives and icons and representations for yourself in your spare time. Look to things that inspire you, that gesture vehemently toward your burgeoning new identity. Prepare for the future marvel that is a recovered you!! (Oh dear, and I promised Jane my publisher that I wouldn't sound like a sucrose, cheesesome proselytising self-help wanker!) Write your own story. Determine novel myths for yourself.

On a personal note, although I concede it is as nutty as hell, I took out a small personal loan to purchase a huge silver and garnet bracelet. It had a kind of Rapunzel/Lady of Shallot ambience. Personally, I was intrigued by the narrative of the woman in the impermeable tower who watched a representation of the world via her mirror and attempted to weave what she saw. I adored the thought of this inviolable beauty stitching the threads of her life back together. Of an impenetrable and lofty duchess making art out of a barely discernible disorder. I was also enamoured of Rapunzel and her long, unapologetically human hair. The whole myth is kind of glorified feminist agoraphobia, I suppose! Whatever the case, I still find great solace in my bracelet. It signifies my past bondage and my present (relative, everything's relative, fellow neurotics!) Liberation. As I fasten it around my wrist I feel secure. I unclasp it when I begin to feel uneasy, as if the mitigation of my anxiety was that simple! It works though. And I've nearly paid the bank back, so fuck it! Oh, and then I took out an even bigger loan and got hair extensions. I am poor and in debt, but discernibly happier. I could not BELIEVE how the hair extensions 'worked' for me. Seven different people have now told me that I have acquired the appearance of a mermaid. Which I like very much, as mermaids, as it happens, are also impenetrable.

You can look to popular culture, classicism, the Tarot or anything you deem appropriate to your needs. As warned by moi in other texts, however, don't go guilelessly window-shopping in other cultures. Not that I believe in it or anything, but it's just bad karma! (Ah, the quaint hypocrisy of my previous statements. Karma, of course, is an imported and purloined concept.) Just be circumspect in your myth-making. Make sure you own your own symbols and subsequent refuge.

Listen to your Panic Attack. What is it trying to tell you? Are any of your symptoms evocative of past memories? And I'm not necessarily talking about the dark, profound, deeply embedded and hideous variety. If you have those, by all means exorcise them at the hands of a capable shrink. You may, however, be able to unwind

Gas *Smells* Awful

the mystery of a particular symptom all by yourself. And thus, of course, begin to thwart it. To employ a FASCINATING personal vignette, I didn't exactly have to wade through layers of subtext to pinpoint the origin of two of my most persistent and debilitating symptoms. For a very long time (and, well, it does happen still) I thought my eyes were going to pop out of my head. As it happens, I'm pretty impoverished in the old vision department. Got over that years ago. Big deal, I'm as blind as a bat. However, on one threshold occasion, the man who was stalking me had been staring at me only metres away for a full hour before I realised he was there. I felt betrayed by my eyes and, as a consequence, they decided to rebel. (I impart this revelation casually, of course, but it did take me months of therapy to work it out!) Second, this parlous event occurred in my place of work. So I felt that my organisation had abandoned me cruelly. I was pissed off that they hadn't even bothered to keep him out for the nth time. As a result, my voice packed up. Seriously, I was talking like a five-year-old girl for around four months. If I wanted to explain a meaty concept, I had to send a note. Talking like an adult was just not a possibility for me. And guess what, I was a radio broadcaster! Known for my shrill confidence, acrid fluently expressed wit and loud harridan's voice, blah blah blah. I had been betrayed by my profession, so I was no longer physically capable of performing my duties. In an odd way, however, these symptoms provided relief. My preoccupation with my eyes forced me to address a real danger; i.e., I couldn't see the loony who was in hot pursuit of me and I needed to make allowances for that. I needed to take binoculars with me wherever I went, a photograph of my stalker or a responsible chaperone. In the end I demanded a bodyguard. It was the only way for me to be truly safe. I wouldn't have considered such extreme measures had my eyes not reminded me to do so. I would have continued to bumble about, visually impaired and threatened, if it were not for the excruciating pain behind my eyes. Further, my broken, intropunitive voice removed me from an occupation that had become nothing but a constant challenge to my health. I mean, I LOVED my job and nothing but these debilitating symptoms could have dragged me away from it. I couldn't talk and, as a result, I couldn't broadcast. In retrospect, my 'decision' to leave work was a very healthy one. Frankly, I was incapable of making such a key life manoeuvre all on my own. My anxiety made me do it! Some months later, I personally thanked my anxiety for taking such exquisite care of me. So some of that weird shit happening to you has a way of eventually making sense.

If you can't hear or read things properly, maybe that's good for the present. Perhaps unpleasant news is just going to make you cry. If you are a student and you can't concentrate on the Hegelian dialectic or something, maybe it would just have driven you to a complicated suicide anyway! If you simply can't handle work, perhaps you shouldn't be there. If you find your partner physically repugnant, perhaps sex and intimate touch is the very last thing you need. Naturally, not every symptom is going to form part of a puzzle. Not every symptom is worth unravelling. Some things don't need to be deconstructed or appraised for their semiotic value. And some symptomatic stuff is just bad for you and you need to try very hard to stop it. For example, not eating, not sleeping or slashing your thighs with a razorblade should not be endured. You and your doctor should fix those things right up! However, it has been my experience that some of my nutty behaviour ended up being useful or, at the very least, instructive. The fact that I was basically blind for about a month was sort of a prophy-lactic. All the horrible things that might have upset me, I just didn't see!

Another exceedingly common symptom is tension in the neck. I have had a number of anxiety attacks which focused on that area. On one occasion I was even positive that my poor abused neck was going to break! A solution came to me one afternoon. I said to myself, 'I'm so sick of holding my head up high!' In the instant I acknowledged that my obsession with appearing dignified was doing me harm, the neck symptoms vanished. I let go of my pride and the extreme neck pain just dissolved. The power of metaphor and suggestion is incredible. I have lost count of the narratives people have proffered to me which describe a symptom and its relation to an incident, a hitherto repressed fear or, amazingly enough, a homily! The Weight Of The World Is On My Shoulders. My Heart Is Breaking. I Want To Stand On My Own Two Feet. Back pain, heart palpitations and unsteadiness can be the actual corollary of the assumptions held 'within' these expressions. Never underestimate the eloquence of your own flesh. Listen to your body. Read the text being written upon it. Think of your flesh and your symptoms as a palimpsest. Understand the messages inscribed upon it. Never be surprised as you discover there are yet more confused hieroglyphics and mixed meanings to decipher. Unlock your body's encrypted messages. I reckon I can lay off this metaphor melange right about now!

Be a Panic Pugilist. At some juncture you're just going to have to get out of bed, turn Patti Smith off the stereo and take your hand out of the Xanax jar. It is inevitable that you will have to fight your panic. As already suggested, don't approach the fight in warrior mode. You are required to be tactical and deceptive rather than bluntly aggressive. To employ boardgames as a conceptual template: we're talking chess here, not battleships! You've got to be more of a Field Marshal Montgomery than a Ghengis Khan. A Sa'aladin rather than a Hussein. Get the picture?

I don't mean that you should simply 'overcome' IT. But you are going to have to look it square in its ugly visage one day and say, 'Hello Panic, Do Your Worst!' There's a time and a place for this tactic, natch! Plan and assess your battle strategy lest you forfeit the success of your personal desert campaign. For example, the aforementioned problem with the eyes still troubles me to the extent that I think I'm going to die. I am still way too frightened to see such an episode to its logical end. But the 'milder' attacks of anxiety I am now able to dismiss by means of a clever challenge. If I am walking down the high street and my heart starts racing and my legs ache to run, I no longer remonstrate with myself. Sometimes I just run. Onlookers be buggered! Sometimes I just let my heart beat at double time. Sometimes I instruct the panic thus 'Okay, You Turd, Get Really Bad. As Terrible As You Can. Go On. Do Your Worst, Bastard. Oh, Is That All You Can Muster? For Fuck's Sake, I Thought I Was Going To Die Last Thursday! THIS IS SO MUCH NOTHING! YOU ARE A TOTAL WUSS! Oh, Shaky Knees And Perspiration. Oh, Nausea And Palpitations. Oh, Like You're So Freddy Krueger. Mister Fucking Scissor Fingers. Hey, Wes Craven Would Pay You SO Much Money To Have You Chase Drew Barrymore Around With A Rusty Garden Implement, Not!' Et cetera.

Gas *Smells* Awful

Dickwitted as it seems, the fact remains that many people can effectively embarrass their anxiety into submission. Challenge it. Please believe me when I tell you that I understand your fear. I know what it is like when your faculty for rational thought packs up, abandons town and leaves you destitute and paralysed in the face of CERTAIN DEATH! Employ restrained and profoundly strategic military tactics. Don't go in for the kill prematurely. Bide your time and get to know thine enemy and/or nemesis and/or *doppelgänger*. The way to fight it is to accede to your vulnerability. I know it sounds trite, but in enhancing one's malleability, one becomes more resilient. Bend with it, don't let it break you. Become pliant, not brittle. Let it happen. Fool it into full flight. Oddly, the more penetrable you become, the more impermeable you become. Yielding works. (Incidentally, blokes should pay A LOT of attention to this last point. We chicks are adept at compromise and openness. You menfolk need to learn about automanipulation and elasticity.)

It could take you an age to be able to enact any of the above suggestions. Some days I just feel so bullied and blunt. Then I just lie and quake in my bed. I quietly loathe myself. I give up. And it appears as if I am either (a) scared that I'm going to die, or (b) planning a way to die. Anxiety and Depression are a mean and probity-deficient pair of shits, aren't they? Just ride it. Accept it. Breathe. Live. That's all you can do.

Always remember that anxiety autoexpresses itself directly through the udder of your poor bruised body! It's a VERY physical experience. So look after yourself, okay? Get some sleep, keep your paw away from sleepy drugs unless you really need them, and do remember to eat.

HELEN RAZER

MY ANXIETY IS DIMINISHING AND, GEE WHIZ, BUT I'M CONFUSED

For me, one of the stickiest junctures en route to (my version of) mental health was, oddly enough, getting better. Let me impart, dearest neurotic, that I had always suspected this would be the case. When anxiety initially set upon me, it became not only my opponent, but my engine. Both my adversary and my *raison d'être*. I guess this is sort of what some women mean when they talk about their codependent marriages. These women posit themselves in an identical relationship to their violent partners as I did to my anxiety. Further, I assume that this is what users experience. They see smack, whiz, vals, moggies, beer or whatever as simultaneous antagonist and saviour. Gamblers, alleged 'sexaholics' and chick friends of mine with a shopping problem all have the same bizarre relationship to their disease.

At the commencement of your breakdown you may find yourself dependent, as I did, on an omnipresent anxiety. I did, in fact, really need my anxiety to get me to work. I needed it to take the bus. If I fixated on my inability to operate, then I'd get so goddamn paranoid that I would, in the initial stages of my acute anxiety disorder, actually do something about it. Strangely, my anxiety made me go to work for eight hours every day. I became used to it. Inured to its vitriol, I suppose. I became so familiar with the sensations of anxiety, I was positive I would be literally unable to breathe without it. I was addicted to anxiety. I was governed by it.

Although, unchecked, it will consume you, anxiety can appear useful. Indeed, it can propel a nutter like you or me toward the shops, the psychiatrist, bus terminus, dentist, school or workplace.

(None of us exists in a socioeconomic vacuum. Sadly. There is always absurd stuff with which we absolutely must wrangle. As previously stated by Helen, Duchess of Admonishment, you should strive, for a time, to avoid those things you loathe. However, I am cognisant of the fact that sometimes you just can't.) You must be very cautious about learning to perceive your panic as a motivator. Anxiety deadens you. Recovery enlivens you.

When I first went to see my shrink, I was very keen on staying at work. As a carefully nonjudgmental sort of psych, he told me that I should really assent to my intuition. That I should do what I felt was best. But he did warn that perhaps mental health was a priority, and that work might be hurting me. In any case, I kept attending work and broadcasting and acting as if very little was wrong. Despite vomiting in the girls' toilet, forgetting my name and generally panicking, I rode on womanfully. Further, I persisted in maintaining what had become a fairly foetid and unhealthy intimate relationship. I convinced myself that if I could only maintain a level of anxiety that ranged from moderate to critical, and not terminal, everything would be just dandy.

Despite my conviction that my anxiety was key and that if I misplaced it everything would fall apart, everything fell apart anyhow! Work turned into an unmitigated disaster. In my anxious and determined state I attracted nothing but critique and the minimum possible volition as far as managerial assistance was concerned. And my relationship ended abruptly when I found my boyfriend contentedly pumping away atop a girl who was ten years younger and ten kilograms lighter than I! While my overt anxiety may have been a fractional catalyst for these events, I do not think it was the point of origin for such everyday tragedy. I'm not saying that my anxiety landed me in more trouble than I could have reasonably expected under 'normal' circumstances. More than likely I would have been banished from work by disapproving management and my boyfriend would have cheated on me anyway. I'm just saying that life continues, regardless of one's anxiety levels.

I was certain that anxiety had provided not only an energy source but a sort of protective pellicle in which I could comfortably drape myself. I know that seems odd. However, do prepare yourself for the irrational fear that you will not be able to function without your anxiety. One may become rooted in the conviction that coping WITHOUT an inability to cope is impossible! If your anxiety starts to scatter and leave you, don't be frightened. Shit is going to happen anyway. Good things, too, will keep occurring. (Although, Goddess knows, there aren't nearly enough pleasant things to satisfy the average neurotic! And those bad things do have a way of piling up when you require them the least! Once again, I'd really like to proffer my unswerving and hefty thanks to the ex who invited some brunette hyperstrumpet to writhe lavishly all over MY brushed Egyptian cotton manchester!) You will, absolutely, be able to function without the ambivalent assistance of your anxiety. In time (and there IS no median time for recovery) you will work, love, eat and generally bumble about without anxiety and with much improved agility.

I do bow to the awful pragmatic truth, however. Sometimes there is stuff that just has to be done. School and work are very tough to avoid. (I was fortunate enough to acquire compensation wages for the greater part of my recovery. However, you can't always hold management solely responsible for your anxiety. I suppose I was 'lucky' to have been emotionally deconstructed at work!) Sometimes the only way you're going to pay your rent, feed yourself or write your essay is by panicking. Sometimes you might have to maintain and embellish the anxiety in order to simply get out of bed.

For so many of us, existence provides us with just two modes of behaviour: depression and anxiety. The former generally precludes the possibility of any action at all. The latter demands action from us, no matter how internally geared and ultimately destructive. Incidentally, I have found that if you supplant one with the other too vehemently, or if you choose to coexist with one disorder at the expense of the other, you just make yourself altogether more fucked up! You must endure both states to conquer them. They are mutually interdependent. Toxically complementary. Or something. The relationship between anxiety and depression is sort of like the misogynist Freudian understanding of the pre-Oedipal stage. Mother and infant bonded in a cruel instant of poisonous mutual absorption. Hey, don't look at me like that! Of course I've been reading Freud on my days off! What else does a grown-up depressive have to do with her time? Anyway . . . anxiety and depression: one does not stir nor lie in wait without the co-operation of the other. So, in short, set aside a little quality time every day for (a) misery and (b) fear! Face each of the evil twins in turn. Then you can begin to thwart them. NEVER resort to one state in the hope that the other will simply go away for ever. If on any given day you choose to endure anxiety, for example, rather than depression, then the depression will just be nourished. You're only giving the depression time off to fester in the shade. Just feel what you feel and don't try to fake it. Don't consciously make yourself experience anything.

Do try to be prescient about your anxiety. Attempt to assess its potential magnitude by chatting with empathetic mates and a decent shrink. If you can attain anything like impartiality about the amount of stress rushing about your body, and if you can make some sterling and precise predictions regarding your potential to completely lose it, act accordingly. Always err on the side of caution!

Anxiety is like a potentially disagreeable child. Certainly it may have some congenital difficulties, but good parenting at a formative stage can quash these tendencies. Be gentle with your anxiety in its infancy. Don't unleash the world on it too soon. It's a precious, overtly sensitive and highly strung little imp and may not be able to attend playgroup with the other toddlers quite so early! The corollary of this twee little analogy is TAKE TIME OFF WORK OR SCHOOL NOW! If possible.

If only I had allowed myself to be an unabashed fruitcake a little earlier, my entire career and professional *raison d'être* and what not would not, perhaps, have been so mightily obliterated.

I had the opportunity (well, several, sadly) to speak with a woman whose experience was a virtual isomer for mine. She had been followed and harassed and irrationally accosted by a loony. Her mode of tolerating and 'managing' the situation was to leave the country. (Moving is very common for the highly anxious. If you have the wanderlust, think twice!) I, by contrast, immersed myself in head-shrinkage within the first three months of hyperdistress. Her irksome experience had occurred five years anterior to the conversation. At this juncture, I had been seeing a cognitive behaviour specialist for just under four months. We were at approximately the same point in our recovery. Although this incident vindicated my decision to be shrunk and prompted a little arrogance from me (golly gee but I was soooo efficient in dealing with my tawdry lot!) I still, of course, wish fervently that I had acted with even greater alacrity. I do despise myself for not leaving my problems in my place of work earlier.

In any case, back to our stated intention. What to do when we are confronted by intimations of emotional health. Embrace the good things. Even though you have become reliant on the consummate torpor that is anxiety, try to remain mutable. If something ridiculous makes you grin, just say FUCK IT and grin.

Chapter *Eight*

First Aid

APART FROM THE INDIGNITY and general discomfort of prolonged emotional chafing and the total absence of a rigorous beauty regimen in your life, I reckon the two worst things about being irresolutely hurled about in the anxiety and depression spin cycle are (a) believing that you're going to die and (b) wanting to die.

I'd just like to attempt to trace the shape of each of these states. Perhaps a narrative or three would be circumspect at this point. And maybe we can begin to devise some emergency procedures.

SO many people deal with the fear of imminent death and the desire to well and truly top themselves. We need to chat about it. If only to keep our hands and collective attention off doing ourselves actual damage.

WHAT TO DO WHEN YOU KNOW THAT YOU'RE GOING TO DIE IN THE NEXT FIVE MINUTES OR SHORTLY THEREAFTER

A short aside, oh sangfroid-deficient fellows! We have to discourse about this fear of death thing. As it happens, there is much yet to be said about the fear of dying. And I fear that I am neither eloquent, recovered nor brave enough to say it! It deserves a book all on its own written by an architect of profound hope who is thoroughly robust and at peace with his/her identity and the world.

If you have endured this conundrum, as I have, I am SO sorry! You do know, don't you, that people don't actually die of acute anxiety? Yeah yeah. It is futile to assure you, I know. You can be a logician capable of reciting pi to infinity, but no-one can guarantee your longevity in the face of total panic. Sometimes you just KNOW that you are going to die.

I haven't any truly tenable solutions, I'm afraid. An overabundant fear of my own mortality is something I deal with at least twice a month. Sometimes it is oppressive beyond expression. And as the very anxious person, in my experience, is generally a beast of extraordinary lexical prowess, there are few things indeed that are beyond the scope of our vocabs!

Feeling like you're about to cark it is horrible. Unspeakably bad. Ineff-ably shite. Some of us feel like we're going to die THIS INSTANT and others are sure they have a terminal disease. Even if our faculty for rational thought and official medical results indicate otherwise. The only possible palliative to this irksome impediment is talk, yet more talk and interpretation. If you can get to the point where you can compare and contrast your fear of death with other neurotics, or at least find a decent person who is committed to understanding your frenzy, you're on your way to relative health.

As I've blathered elsewhere, I have often assumed that I was moribund when experiencing certain symptoms. First, my eyes plagued me. I genuinely believed that they were going to pop out of my head and unleash lavish gallons of cerebral fluid. Second, I still occasionally suspect that my neck is going to break. Innumerable people have told me that they feel as though they will have a heart attack. Others are certain that someone is trying to kill them. A close female relative of mine enduring acute anxiety disorder simply KNEW she was going to die. She had not even bothered to develop a fictitious rationale for her demise. She would just sit there, quaking and crying and screaming, 'I'm going to die!'

A friend, who insists she was not suicidal at all, was wrangling with profound anxiety as the result of her sister's death. She was terrified of dying at her own hand. Although, she conveyed to me, she did not WANT to die, she was positive that she would transform into a self-annihilating automaton and simply do herself in with a carving knife as her rational portion looked on in sheer disbelief.

Some people report sensations of physical disintegration. Others just KNOW they have cancer. Ostensibly lucid people become uncomfortably assured that the municipal water is poisoned, that their companion animal will suffocate them as they slumber, or that a great big old craggy yawning maw in the earth will suddenly and inexplicably appear and chew them up whole.

Whether we have developed an elaborate reason for our fear of mortality or not, it still frightens the bejesus out of us. What to do, oh my brood of similarly disfurnished pusscats?

I have discovered that talking myself out of this phobia simply does not work. The more pressure I put on my faculty for reason, the more polluted that part of my brain seems to get. I just become one big old phrenic mess and LOSE IT. Anxiety is a fluid and fascistic foe when it jolly well feels like it. It seeps EVERYWHERE and claims EVERYTHING. The manner in which anxiety can claim every conceivable intellectual function is quite confounding. Frankly, if I attempt to assert some antidote to anxiety, the damn voracious monster just appears to get more agitated. It colonises every filament of my notional being and manages to make a short meal of anything like rationalism or 'perspective'.

So maybe, rather than administering a stern lecture to yourself, just let it happen.

A little cajolery can work to mitigate the fear of death on occasion. I sometimes proffer sucrose blandishments to my anxiety behemoth. This seems to work nicely if I'm at home in bed or somewhere else alone and 'safe'. I tell the anxiety something along the lines of, 'Look, wouldn't this be much more fun for you if you tried it, say, on Thursday when I have to go to the shrink? You could grab me by the throat at the train station and, with any luck, you'll terrify me so much that I'll actually urinate right there on the platform in front of a whole bunch of strangers?' I urge my anxiety to assess its own efficacy. I insist that such torment is a waste of its time. I tell it to save its strength. You know, pop off, sharpen your claws and set upon me at the most inappropriate time? As a fairly primal, thick as shit beast, anxiety sometimes buys my entreaty and goes away.

Another thing to try is simply moving around. If you can't get out of bed, just have a little roll. Pull your hair. Touch your toes. DO ANYTHING to remind yourself that there is a frame of reality anterior to the advent of your anxiety and fear of death. Well, do *just about* anything! Self-flagellation, vomiting or cutting yourself up are not recommended. Affirmations, as dickwitted as they are, are occasionally effective. Something banal and pastel and gross as in 'I

Accept Myself' can work a treat. (Just don't let anyone you respect hear you! Even though we feel like we're going to die, we don't want to compromise our integrity now, do we?) Between us, the Alcoholics Anonymous serenity prayer seemed to soothe me. (You know, 'God grant me the Serenity to accept the things I cannot change . . . Courage to change the things I can and Wisdom to know the difference . . .) I just substituted the 'God' part of it with 'chocolate', 'Two Fat Ladies' or something I actually believed in and adored that day. The appropriation thing again, of course. Refer to the relevant passage!

The performance of obsessive and quaint little rites can function ably too. The magick thing. I'm always recovering some warped hex hypertext on the world wide web. In more pitiable moments, I can often be observed binding, protecting and chanting. A little odd as, being a resolute postmodern and all (yes, I know a self-professed postmodern subject cannot be resolute), I don't actually believe in much of anything at all. Particularly not witchcraft! I never expected to turn to paganism in my extended hour of dire need, but I never predicted that I'd be shivering in my lonely bed awaiting my own lavish finale, either. Extreme circumstance demands extreme medicine.

These days, as the mortal panic attacks occur less frequently, I turn increasingly to my security blanket. Even for the nihilist or existentially minded, when anxiety and fear of death come crashing into your life, you need SOMETHING to believe in. So at times I worship my previously mentioned bracelet. It hitches me to a particular time and sensation. It functions as an emblem of my berth in sanity, my indelible will to recuperate and my ability to actually go to the shops! A nice (formerly bulimic and relentlessly anxious) person I know actually purchased a little silver charm in the shape of an anchor. She wears it in her navel, under her clothes. When she detects the need to be moored in some kind of sense, she fondles it. She wears it in her tummy to remind herself that she needs to take care with her diet and lower colon. I wear my excessive bracelet on my right hand owing to the psychiatric assumption that this hand is governed by the left side of my brain. I muse, in my odd and overabundantly involute way, that my left and logical lobe is empowered by this simple gesture. I have inscribed my own mythology upon the rational part of my poor battered person, I think. It makes me feel as though I am coinciding with myself. I am whimsical and sensible both, I insist to myself when I tinker with the big old medieval-looking thing. Logic and Disorder comfortably co-exist. Or at least that's the shit I spin. So what? It works.

Oh. Never underestimate the power of trustworthy underpants. New tattoos, a novel hair colour, pictures, CDs and wind chimes all may contain transformative power. Again, spend some time musing and figuring out an all new symbolic order for yourself. A minor change can be as good and as potent as a holiday at the funny farm. Play with your suggestibility. If something as dumb as dirty dishes can convince you that you're about to meet your cruel and sarcastic maker, then maybe a little trinket or a tiny, twisted and jolly manoeuvre such as the purchase of a dewy-finish high quality face foundation is capable of transmuting you into a more content little neurotic. You are, obviously, emotionally malleable. Run with it. Allow yourself tiny pleasures. If you are being moved to ecstasy by silly little things, please revel in the lascivious and evanescent rush. Don't give yourself shit for finding extreme joy in odd places.

Gas *Smells* Awful

I know a lot of doctors with titanium credentials would disagree with me on this last point. Their therapeutic objective is often to render us more emotionally moderate. They often suggest that to travel from dire unhappiness to golden joy is bad and naughty and distinctly unhealthy. I say fuck it. And I'm sorry about that. I deem it essential to maintain some experience, however fleeting, of joy. What do the French call it? *Jouissance.* A very groovy and ambiguous word. Defies translation but does suggest, according to some, a spasm or attack of happiness. It also gestures toward the sheer physicality of happiness. We don't have a word like it. Anyway, it is, I assert, key to retain some link with contentment. It is SO easy for a depressive to forget the shape and the texture and the taste of joy. It's dangerous to forget! I believe it is wrong-headed for us to deny ourselves even the merest, most insubstantial filament of *jouissance.* Our bodies need to be reminded what it feels like. Our muscles desperately require the memory of it. And, you know, although we may think of ourselves as emotionally bisected, extreme or manic, I don't think this is always the case. Often, although the brief fling with joy will appear to be extreme, it just bloody might not be. Sometimes our experience of happiness just appears to be radical and defiant and manic. Sometimes what we depressives and anxious fruitbats perceive as ecstasy may merely manifest as mild contentment in a more 'normal' replete-with-serotonin type individual. Those purportedly dangerous intimations of happiness may just be fits of something like health. I know that on occasion you may feel an unwieldy great crushing love for a dear little pusscat, for example. I think that depression and anxiety can quite simply decontextualise quite tenable and sensible and 'decent' emotions. Basically, we walk about feeling so shit that when happiness strikes, it may be so unfamiliar as to be unfeasible. I just recommend that you don't arm yourself against it. Enjoy it while it lasts. Life is comprised of much crap. Cling tenaciously to the good stuff!

Just go with it, finally. Ride the wave and when it dumps you, be prepared. Embellish your material and mental arsenal against fear and be assured, PLEASE, that you will live through this. (Which reminds me, *Live Through This* from Hole is an excellent recovery soundtrack! Well, it was until I started buying those trance cassettes.) Now that we've conquered the fear of dying, we're so damnably exhausted and down that we probably want to kill ourselves anyway. So . . .

HOW DO I NOT KILL MYSELF?

Okey dokey, then. I should impart from the outset that I've tried it. Couple of times, more than likely. Fortunately, for me, women are notoriously unsuccessful where topping themselves is concerned. I just took way too many pills, vomited a lot and went to sleep for a month or something. Yes, I am just a fractal image made flesh. I am the reification of chaos theory and I'm an utter hopeless git who couldn't even get killing herself bloody right. Honestly, though, I did want to die. Or rather, I wanted to sleep for the remainder of my life. Actually, I wanted to vow silence, never be rubbed by another person again, keep in textual touch with a few select people via my laptop, eat nothing but breakfast cereal, wake up for an hour a day and watch substandard pay per view. I wanted to reside in a kind of pop culture purgatory, I suppose. I just wanted stasis. I wanted passivity, endless rest and no challenges. I wanted the impossible. So, as a pragmatist, I conceded that I'd have to earn a wage and that such a scheme was untenable. How then would I pay the internet service provider? Who would buy my Cocoa Pops? How could I maintain such a state if I couldn't face the thought of the pharmacist? So suicide seemed like the next best option. No matter how assiduously and passionately I addressed the eternal interrogation, 'What is the fucking point and why do I fucking bother?', I could not synthesise a substantial retort.

Frankly—and again I apologise on behalf of the misshapen cosmic grid—there is no answer. Or rather, the answers are confusing and hard won. My quest for meaning across the years led me to Friedrich Nietzsche's *Thus Spake Zarathustra* and Jean Paul Sartre's *Being and Nothingness*. And then all the other tossers I have mentioned. Admittedly, and regrettably, I was too much of a disgruntled manurehead at the time to pick up on all the epistemic nuances. What I did learn, living in the pellicle of my suicidal distress, was that we beasts are capable of metamorphosis. Big deal, I hear you gasp. However, change is key. Change is intriguing. It provides an answer, of sorts.

For various reasons (try-hard intellectual elitism not least among them!) I tend to turn to continental philosophers in times of trouble. You may not be so inclined. However, as mentioned elsewhere in this fractured tract, I firmly believe that one faculty which is not negatively affected by anxiety and/or depression is that which holds onto abstract thought. Or rather, the recovery period that immediately follows anxiety and depression helps you to consider the Really Big Questions. As I have said. Again and again. But it bears repeating. I have NEVER met an ex-depressive or former anxious nut-bar who did not emerge from their ordeal with anything less than discernibly improved conceptual dash. Strange little bonus, this one. Set upon your enhanced ability to think about the Big Questions. Hell, you're going to anyway! You are consistently occupied with those questions that bothered the ancients so much. Who Am I? Why Do I Exist? Do I Really Exist? And, For That Matter, What's This Thing For?

It really can help to set aside the .38 special for an instant, push the kilogram of recently purchased scag to the back of the contraband medicine cupboard and read, if only for a few minutes a day. Plato, Descartes, Aquinas, Spinoza, Hegel, Derrida, Foucault, Barthes, Kristeva or Irigaray. Anybody who ruthlessly tackles the meatiest problems. Personally, I found great solace in the postmoderns. Particularly Roland Barthes. First, it's a fuckload easier to read than some of that other scary French shit. Second, Barthes explains 'reality' as being the waste product of language. As someone who sleeps with a dictionary by her bed and won't even consider having sex with anyone unless they can use an apostrophe correctly, Barthes's emphasis on language and signification really worked for me.

It was mostly the putatively nihilistic philosophers who altered my perspective. I always liked the 'Well, we don't really exist, so let's party!' school of thought. (Look, if you're a PhD in hermeneutics or some shit, bugger off. I can reduce the entire rich history of continental thought to a single dumb sentence if I want!) And Nietszche for me was always a kind of 'Let's party with a new yet responsible attitude to "morality" and be strong and clever' kind of guy. As a sensitive leftie type, I could never cope with a total absence of political principles. I mean, sometimes you just have to be considerate and just. So Friedrich kind of worked for me on that score. Without evincing didacticism, he managed to lead me to a conceptual place where I found I was making 'fair' decisions about the world and my place within it. His entire 'overcoming' and turning into your own deity and looking at the world as an exciting abyss really did it for me. (Please don't worry that his work was poached and acculturated by the Nazis. They got it so wrong! Nietzsche has helped a lot of very decent people. I swear!)

I know, if you're looking for a reason to exist, the whole existential trip might make you feel ill. Helen, I'm Perilously Close To Eating Razorblades On Toast And You're Telling Me That I Don't Exist? Sorry. If you are the bookish type in search of a reason to live, I would suggest reading Sartre's *Nausea* in an effort to embrace and be empowered by your uncertainty. You CAN get to a conceptual site where the never-ending quest for meaning in the face of chaos actually EXCITES rather than deadens you. Also, Camus' *The Myth of Sysiphus* is widely available and pretty good for enhancing that 'rejoicing in the texture of that which is apparently fucked' feeling.

Then again, you might like to try reading more orthodox books. *The Republic* or something. If you feel you need someone who explains everything, don't bother with any twentieth century philosophers. They're just in a total notional muddle! If you are enchanted, as I have been, by contemporary thinkers, buy the *Oxford Dictionary of Philosophy* or some cheat notes first. Go to the primary texts later. Start simple, get compelled and then go about devising your very own reason to live. For some, the whole reading trip can work. Even when you're on the very edge of self annihilation.

Writing (rather obviously!) also continues to provide me with a sense of solace. Any medium, really, that enables you to depict, change, reflect, explain, bend or break reality can work. Art galleries can help. Music. Anything with loads of texture. Anything polysemous. Anything grand and complex. Any pursuit which demands your response, phrenic creativity or ideas can assist you in refraining from suicide. Refer to my other shite about appropriation and better health.

Now, all this sub-academic crap is all very well and good, isn't it? But what happens when you can't read? Sylvia Plath documents her experience of temporary illiteracy in *The Bell Jar*. Often, profoundly literate types will find that their reading and writing skills just go on a beagle-style roam. (By contrast, folks previously disinterested in 'high concept' literature may well develop a taste for it upon the occasion of their temporary insanity!) So, what to do then?

Well, you should jolly well have an emergency number for your shrink, first of all. Also, if you're on the brink, you might want to consider going to hospital. I did that once. After two hours of sitting in casualty like a total dill, I bored myself into wanting to live. Of course, you do run the risk of being scheduled under some mental health act or other if you present to a particularly feisty triage type. So be warned.

Oh, and I should mention Lifeline and various online services. However, I have never used these facilities myself. Others do tell me that they can provide useful assistance. There's information on numbers and sites for these facilities at the back of this book.

You might wish to consider NOT ringing your parents or significant other. First, sometimes they don't need to hear that someone they love is on the verge. Their (understandably) histrionic reaction might just make you feel worse. More desperate, more tangled and more responsible for everything that has ever gone wrong in the history of meaning. If you have a friend who has admitted harbouring similar dank desires, call them. Fortunately, I have one woman in my life to whom I can comfortably impart, 'I want to die' and she'll generally respond with something along the lines of, 'Yeah, I felt like that this afternoon. It's a bitch, isn't it?' It makes me feel less pompous. I become less involved in the drama of my own self-loathing. It may appear as an odd suggestion, but if you can be more laconic and generally casual and accepting of your suicidal impulse, the desire just might disappear. I do believe that as suicide and the overwhelming will of many people to enact it becomes a more acceptable topic of polite conversation, our desire for it will dwindle. Lacan or some French dude said something along the lines of 'a thing is more powerful when it is veiled'. Nietzsche said something about 'it being invisible hands that torment us'. When desire is denuded and described, it will often dissolve, quite simply. So I do wish more folks would chat competently and logically about their absolute NEED to kill themselves. It really is so damn widespread. We must learn to accept that such thoughts are almost inevitable. Being the only beasts, perhaps, on the planet who bear knowledge of their own mortality, of course we're going to think about things like dying and agency and stuff. In short, you have to think, 'I affirm the fact that I want to kill myself. This is a normal feeling. I accept myself regardless. Now, where did I put my Prozac?' It is perfectly fine and normal to entertain thoughts of suicide. Actually doing it, however, is a bit whacked. So don't. Particularly if you have borrowed this book from a library. Someone else might want to read it, you selfish bastard.

Avoid being theatrical and garish and romantic about the whole deal. Suicide does have great cultural cachet. It's a bit like strong Marlboros, punk rock or heroin. Or motorcycles perhaps. I remain convinced that many youngsters top themselves because they think it's hip. Not for a nanosecond, to mitigate or deride the intensity of the feeling. However, suicide is a very Nick Cave meets James Dean meets Emily Bronte pastime. (NB, young impressionable suicidals: NONE of these exceptionally iconoclastic personages killed themselves. Okay? And a jolly good thing too. What if the 'Mercy Seat' had never been sung? Where would I be without *Wuthering Heights*? Well, actually, probably in a decent relationship instead of perpetually single with dark menacing rock and roll Heathcliff type interludes. Thanks a lot for fetishising self-embracing, insensitive, rugged, poorly washed loners with long hair, Emily. No, I really appreciate that. Thanks.)

In many cases I believe suicide constitutes a rebellious act. The orthodox understanding of topping oneself would state that the act is characterised by thorough isolation. People tend to think of suicide as a process where the fact of other people pales into irrelevance. Personally, when I imagined my own death (and subsequent tasteful funeral attended, no doubt, by very A list guests all dressed in trim little Emporio Armani suits and sombre, vastly respectful DEVASTATED guilty expressions on their flawlessly made-up visages) it was always in a very stylised, soft-focus mode. And without fail I would imagine how I would be fitfully and fondly remembered for years to come. Those who had trivialised my pain,

I imagined, would FINALLY have to confront the consequence of their arrant stupidity! I would be shriven and they would be punished! And we'd all be very well-dressed.

On certain murky days I would imagine my special suicide outfit. The austere Von Troska cocktail shift or the Third Millennium slip? Or, damn it all, should I actually buy something new as, after all, I wouldn't have to bear the credit card consequences? Should I apply Chanel's winter colour palette to my face or draw my last breath *sans maquillage*, with just a dash of my perennial favourite Poppy Inspiration lip colour? Hair down like a shroud, framing my pallid visage, or up in a deconstructed Bardot knot to display the new fragility of my white neck? Should I consult my hair stylist? Should I scatter relevant weighty and culturally diverse texts about my person just to ensure that everyone knew I was very fucking deep? And clever, natch. Golly gosh, but I did bumble about for a while looking so fucking fey and desperate.

In planning my suicide I was almost completely motivated by how other people would think of me when I was dead. About how I would be found arranged symmetrically on my neat bed with prim little slits in my wrists. The tiny red aperture in my arm, the fit, man! fiendishly close to my gorgeous and well dressed corpse. Hasn't she got thin? they would say. Why didn't we notice? they would reprimand themselves. Oh so delicate, physically and spiritually both. Let us celebrate her evanescence. WHAT A SPECIAL GIRL! Shortly thereafter, my incisive bitter poetry would be discovered. I'd not only be vindicated and forgiven for my neuroses, but I would be celebrated in my demise. In proffering my own death to the world, I reasoned, I had begun to rewrite my life. What a sad imp. It is odd, isn't it, how we sometimes think about suicide as a positive change rather than the dull, dumb, ugly and thoroughly motiveless act that it is.

Even if you don't think about accessorising your suicide with the same obsessive panache as I, I'll bet you've thought about your funeral, haven't you? Stirring eulogies, discerning floral arrangements and *Goin' To California* resounding wetly from the stereo. The deadhouse would be replete with devastated, guilty and nicely turned-out mourners. Aaah, the men in pin-striped Zegna suits! The women wrapped in Colette Dinnigan and grief! The fretful, elegant notes that would accompany me to the grave. (Cremation was rarely an option for me while inhabiting my richly textured suicide fantasy realm. I was born a Catholic, after all. And the poignant inverted symbolism of my body returning to earth seemed way too delicious to give up. I made my will. Sadly, however, I am the last Macintosh user on earth. So I hope the format preferences of my last will and testament are not lost when someone converts the zip drive to a Windows system. What if all bold and italicised text is gobbled up by Bill Gates's insatiable binary maw? You have to think about this stuff!)

If, like me, you think about suicide as constituting some form of revenge, forget it! You know how easily we forget school friends and ex-colleagues? Despite well-formed intentions, they simply dissolve from our memories. The fact is, despite our collective Western obsession with nostalgia, you'll be easily forgotten by the masses. Think about all the people you have met. No matter how dearly you loved or admired them, they are laid to rest in your memory merely as vague remnants. Ponder that before you top yourself. Give the bastards a week or two and they'll be back being productive and laconic and happy. It's not that you're irrelevant, of course. However, humans appear to be capable of resiling from the greatest hardship. Your death, no matter how violent and well-planned, will eventually emerge as an incident. A parlous chapter in the narrative of someone else's life. Actually, more like a footnote than a chapter! A bloody bibliographical entry. If you want to kill yourself to (a) effect conceptual mortality or (b) really piss some people off, you will NOT be rewarded.

And the truth is, no-one looks good dead except for Nosferatu. And he is a goddamn fictional character. Not even Marilyn Monroe looked decent as a corpse. Blood-letting is messy and it cheeses people off and it will ruin your outfit. Apparently, the act of hanging oneself can cause the evacuation of (ah hum) Certain Bodily Secretions. Yuck. Pong. Gas makes you blue and splotchy. Heroin and pills make you chunder all over your bib. For the less vertiginous amongst you, think twice before you jump. Do you have any idea how messy and disembodied and not like you at all you're going to look when they recover your bits? Drowning, however modish, is (a) very difficult to achieve and (b) unflattering in the extreme. I have fought against retaining water my entire adult life! I'm not going to leave a bloated cadaver for people to laugh at! As for death by self-administered gun fire, did you SEE those pictures of poor Kurt Cobain on the net? What a dog's breakfast that was. There is no fashionable and becoming suicide option.

Further, even if your death is a relatively 'peaceful' and pretty one, corpses have a tendency to look nothing at all like their living tenants. I remember in high school that a friend's aunt died of some virulent cancer. My comrade was perturbed by the thought that she would have to respect family tradition and view the body of her dead favourite aunt. She had assumed that it would be too vivid. She was terrified that she would be fitfully reminded of the woman that she had loved. She said to me one morning at recess, 'You know, now I know why they call a corpse "The Body". I looked at her and she wasn't there. She wasn't the person I knew. She was just some rotting thing.' No matter how much of a spunk you are, you're not going to look your ethereal best when dead.

If, like me, you cradle a neo-Gothic aesthetic within and reckon you are going to come across all Percy Bysshe and tastefully consumptive in death, you are so wrong. Find some real photos of pre-mortician dead people. They're not pretty.

Although it may seem like a fabulous idea, suicide is just a pointless ineffective bloody waste of time. Remember this when you veer toward it. Please try to learn to accept the desire to kill yourself. And don't be tethered by it. Don't let that powerful thought define you, okay? Think about it, sure. You're probably going to anyway. And BELIEVE ME, I understand why it might seem like a viable option. But please don't get caught up in the sexiness and romance of it all. Please don't be afraid to acknowledge that you feel this way. It's NORMAL to think about it. So normal. And it's also normal to get intoxicated by the thought of it. It's normal to feel seduced by the notion of one big sleep. Sometimes I find it DELICIOUS to think about. On certain days the temptation of suicide hovers about me like the promise of an eternity spent in a five star hotel. Indulge in such a fantasy, if you must. But don't merge with it, if you see what I mean. Don't become so entangled by the perversity and attractiveness of it that it informs everything you do. Get to the point where you can simply recognise it and intone, 'Gosh, I'm having a suicidal thought.' And when it's gone, let it go. Don't feel like a coward or a heel or a great pretender if you don't get around to doing it. Feel relief! When you are frolicking near the brink, clutch one of those things that may make you happy. Let it cajole you.

Finally, you really should have learned by now that all things are malleable, fluid and subject to great change. Your moods are capricious. The urge will pass. Your mood will alter. You will resile. And the shape of your life, too, is relentlessly shifting. Stick around to watch things unfurl. Wear your depression and your seemingly indefatigable urge to top yourself like a shroud when you must. Accept that tomorrow you may very well feel as naked, naïve and as full of kicking promise as a new cat. Things move. Stay around to chart their progress.

Read. Find people you can talk to about suicide openly and with some levity. Read about it. Paint bloody pictures or make dioramas out of it. Write shit-house poetry. Anything. Forge endless justifications for it, if you must. Just bloody don't bloody do it. NO-ONE WILL BE IMPRESSED.

Chapter *Nine*

The Unspeakable Horror of Other People

D EAR WORLD, WROTE I one miserable afternoon, *Dear World, although I am strong, dear world, I prefer to avoid situations that demand my strength. Although I can ably accept anything you might like to hurl at me, I prefer to be able to duck in advance. Although I am resilient, I prefer not to have to resile. But you shouldn't worry that much. I mean, fire away. All my expectations are uncommonly low and my vulnerability is locked away. You can't hurt me. You should know this before we become any more involved. Thanks. Helen.*

I wrote a lot of stupid crap like that. I always managed to come across as some fey anorexic Vaucluse princess who is preparing to be dumped. It was in this delicate, ladylike style that I apprehended the majority of persons when I was recovering. I was a bit of a fragile girlfriend to the world. I *was* unusually susceptible to the mode in which people treated me. However, I wanted to let them know that although I was aggrieved and afraid and all at sixes and sevens generally, ultimately I would survive. That although I seemed pathetic, I wasn't. That really, I jolly well led a full, busy and intriguing life and had lots of friends and fabulous diversions and autonomy and unlimited credit. (Which of course I didn't. Don't!) Or something. I suppose, like a simpering girlish idiot on the verge of being jilted, I wanted to let him know that his victory over me was pyrrhic. I wanted to inform him that, while I was temporarily stung by his rejection or abandonment or cruelty, no permanent imprint could be left. I did not want people to rejoice in my susceptibility. I did not want them to enjoy my pain. I wanted to let them know that it was all rather evanescent, as far as I was concerned. That they could trammel and harm me for no longer than a nanosecond. That by Friday night I would have bought a new dress, completed an assiduous toilette and emerged on the streets of inner Sydney with some young brattish spunk attached to my simulated Prada heels by a harness. Possibly a little silly. But to write and ponder such things helped. Still helps.

That's my first filament of warped advice. Imagine the world to be a cruel, egoistic self-embracing lover by whom you are still a little entranced. Get in and dump him or her before they can do it to you. Listen to the sage advice of mother and sober friends. 'He's no good for you. Get out of that relationship before you lose your self-respect and CD collection!' That's what I reckon anyway.

But how do we really ignore idiots en masse? How do we deal with the peril, ignorance and fuckwittage of others? Well don't look at me. Who am I anyway, Deepak Bloody Love Everybody Chopra? My post-traumatic shit list reads like a Who's Who of incendiary fuckwits. Ah, the friendships I have lost, the relationships I have poisoned with my anxious tantrums. The total turds who failed the acid test of devotion. Fuck them all.

Unhappily, we do all have to deal with fucksticks. With their snobbery, bemusement, panic, nescience, repulsion, ardent self-interest and general free-floating nastiness. We may have to also steel ourselves against their cloying concern, their bad advice, their contempt and their absurd suggestions. We may have to hear 'I don't know what you're so worried about', 'Just relax!' or 'Come on, put on a happy face' more than we care to recall. Ah, the ignominy and pain of it all, kids!

Let us first confront the:

SHEER UNMITIGATED FUCKWIT

Easy to recognise and impossible to bear. There are those who may feel it is their duty to treat you like total shit. Some people actually think that disdain is good for you! And there are others still who may allow their malevolence to emanate from jealousy. Some people will actually think that you, in all your emotional disarray, are being indulgent! They are aghast that you dare to achieve what they long for. Yes, some people are actually JEALOUS of your discord!! And then there are plain old garden-variety pricks who just think you're an idiot for letting it all unravel. Oh, and there are those who are pissed off that you are no longer an immutable, dependable, armoured sanity beast. They are simply cheesed that you can't come out to play any more. Whatever. They are all just sheer unmitigated fuckwits and they must be dealt with in fairly much the same manner regardless of their particular fuckwit hue.

What do we do? First, get them the fuck out of your life! And if you can't, pretend you are an anthropologist. Mum and I have been doing this for years at irksome and compulsory social functions.

We pretend that we are both Margaret Mead. You know, that woman who went to PNG or something and got everything wrong? That is us. Constantly misinterpreting, reinventing and problematising an alien culture. We imagine ourselves to be on a quest for meaning. We become so intrigued by the intricacies of local dialogue, national dress and bizarre customs (such as that, at weddings, of the best man turning into a drunk and sexist anus) that we outrun depression and potential anxiety. If we have downed enough chablis and shite function champagne, as is quite often the case, we will also take notes. I actually completed three years of social anthropology as part of my (incomplete and totally thematically warped) Bachelor of Arts in order to embellish this pretence. Mother and I are now able to brandish legitimate ethnographic terms such as 'moiety', 'bride price', 'Kula ring', 'Levi-Strauss', 'ethnocentric', 'Malinowsky', 'infibulation', 'functiono- structuralism' and 'fuck this do is really shitting me' with great confidence and conviction. Such is the power of our lexicon and the depth of our fancy that people generally leave us alone. Well, that and the fact that we are generally so rat-arsed by telegram time that everyone is apprised of our destructive potential. They know it is best to allow us our fractured solitude!

In any case, I suggest that you try assuming the position of the valiant, pith-helmeted ethnographer. You are not an actual participant where fuckwits are concerned. You are a participant-observer. You are only partially immersed. Your involvement only extends to a delimited degree. You do not feel superior to these people. Quite simply, you have not yet learned their language. Their rites still bemuse you. You are grappling to understand them. They are a mystery. You are compiling your fully funded anthropological doctorate in the Land Of The Fuckwits. You are shortly to emerge as a Doctor of Complete And Utter Arseholes. People will rejoice and gasp at the effulgent bon mots and musing to be found within your dissertation 'Traversing Fuckwitania'.

Honestly. This smug (and partially elitist) little trick really can work. Tell yourself, I Am Only Here To Take Notes.

If highly structured fantasy is not your bag, there are other less involved ways to remove yourself from undesirable contacts. As an anxious chickadee, you are rather adept at the old 'stepping outside oneself' trick, no? Use the pain of depersonalisation as an advantage. Step right outside yourself and look with unclouded objectivity (if there is such a thing, which there isn't, but who cares?) and ponder, why is this person being such a shit to me? Isn't it fascinating how the mentally unwell are treated? Watch the terror unfurl in their eyes. Watch yourself reflected in their gaze. Stare as their terror of you, expressed as hate or mendacity, encroaches. I know this sounds wan and silly and like I'm feeding you a big old smelly nose bag of reject horse weed, but do think: I am so much better off than this poor dickwit. You are! Absolutely. You have already confronted theories and modes of being human which they can barely approach. You have been to the bottom and you have survived. This person before you who so roundly despises your illness is just jealous of where you have been and where you will, inevitably, end up. They are thinking: this is one brave fucker. Why can't I have a hissy fit and three shrink appointments a week too?

Become a sociologist if you will (although one despises this blank discipline) when terror strikes. You are attempting to assess the manner in which loonies are marginalised and feared. How are we treated? Why are we so repulsive yet magnetic? If you want an analogy to begin with before the commencement of your study, think of sexism or racism. 1. Sexism. Certain poorly trained gents fear women. The really rotten blokes detumesce in the presence of a comfortably womanly woman. They lash out as their metaphoric organs contract. Basically, their dicks shrivel and they get all bitchy and turn! Misogynists are envious of a woman's comfort with her body, her ability to construct solutions from several different and simultaneous standpoints and her general otherness. 2. Racism. Similarly, racist arseholes fear black folks. Or whomsoever is their enmity *de jour*. The white racist despises what he/she assumes to be the black person's comfort with their sexuality, verbal fluency and general wild and free otherness. (Obviously, all these 'qualities' are white-fuelled constructs and not necessarily the case.) The racist or pompous sexist git is not dissimilar to the professedly sane madophobic. We nut-bars represent, as do women and marginalised others, a gap in their order. We represent the underbelly, the other side, the ghastly reflection, the unadorned chaotic truth, the blood, the organs, the intuition, the beginning, the end, the waste, the 'stuff' of the universe or whatever you like! We constitute the uncomfortable excess. Essentially, we just don't fit in. It's xenophobia, kids. You simply have to learn to handle it now you're a citizen of loonyland.

For those such as me who have learnt to accept and work their gross difference as a matter of course, the aforementioned acceptance comes rather easily. I, for example, was (and remain) a deathly pale girl with poor and noncorrectable eyesight and no sporting prowess. I am, and always was, an ardent feminist. I am, and always was, thanks to my fabbo parents, a vocal antiracist. I like books. I adore strange clothes and dark nail-varnish. I am unable to contain my strangeness. If you are not, and never have been, one of us, learn to love it! If you are peachy keen and picture-perfect, embrace the opportunity to learn what it is like for us, the daggy disenfranchised constituency of loser, slacker, vampiric bookworms. Hey, former jocks and jockettes, there IS a reason that *The Catcher in the Rye* and *The Bell Jar* remain bestselling texts. Our exclusion from the middle makes us fascinating. Our enforced solitude and subterfuge forces us to read, to seek and to write very bad poetry indeed.

If people are avoiding you because of your panic attacks and untenable depression, fuck 'em. You don't want them. Seek out the punk rock profligates instead. Search for the sad little girl with the pierced elbow reading Emma Goldman in her grandmother's mourning dress and ask her if you can compare scars! Look for the ostracised Slayer devotee in the office who has scrawled 'Inflicted' on a Post-It note and stuck it to his acne-spattered forehead. Remain vigilant lest you miss the Dungeons and Dragons devotee and all her sterling neuroses, the bleak aspirant performance artiste and the articulate self-loathing of the Java-literate uber-geek. We are the best fucking people you will ever know. We are the ones who will stick around. Moreover, we are the folks who will find you the most fascinating at your nadir. Learn to embrace us. Watch how we do things. Don't ever abandon us. We have very long memories!

Seriously, though, you are just going to have to give up the A-list pretensions and claim your Dark Continent citizenship. As quickly as possible. One of us. One of us. Tee hee. Really, you do have my sympathy, you formerly perfectly formed neo-neurotic, you! It must be crap to be fabulous one day and despised by all the cool kids the next. You really do have to educate yourself in the precise art of otherness, though. You are not one of the seamless pure-hearts any more. You are an oddball. And even after recovery, an oddball you shall remain.

Give up your chic. Relinquish your social standing. I know it can pain a formerly desirable boy or girl. And don't think I don't understand. My own little breakdown was, more than likely, more highly publicised and gossiped about than yours! I felt like a total idiot. I went from consisting in some (shabby) punk rock celebrity milieu and gainful employment to NOTHING. A reject. Effluent. Et cetera. So, whatever. You are just going to have to accede to your new life in the shadows. You must now accept and fitfully adore your difference. As inadvisable as some clever folk with letters after their name may find this advice, you must develop pride! You must wear the relentless scorn of others as a badge of honour. You must quietly collect their antagonistic scalps and hang them from your belt!

Prepare yourself for rejection. For you will be rejected. So many people avoided me as though I were infectious. And that is the other thing, oh newly marginalised! They DO think that you are pestilence! They don't want to catch you or your disease. This fear may be the source of the Sheer Unmitigated Fuckwit's poor treatment and evasion of you. And in some cases, you have to understand. And you have to cease thinking of them as a Sheer Unmitigated Fuckwit. A former dear friend of mine still does not really talk with me, post hissy fit. This person cannot deal with any intimation of craziness because an immediate family member suicided during a bout of manic depression. This person is shriven, as far as I can Messianically grant that kind of grace! Their fear needs to be respected and understood. They are terrified that the 'illness' is immanent within them. Any intimate proximity with me—and I am still an 'out' outpatient and proud neurotic—brings the fear and the memories back to them far too lucidly. Fortunately, this frightened person had the decency and valour to inform me of all this. Their name has been excised from the shit list! From my experience and that of others, I warn that the chances are high someone will give you an unreasonably hard time. Just ignore them. They do not exist. You cannot hear them.

THE SHEER UNMITIGATED FUCKWIT AT SCHOOL AND IN THE WORKPLACE

There are certainly those, often in the workplace, who will unambiguously demand that you do not bring your Little Problems to work, thanks. Well, obviously, as much as we'd love to, we can't tuck the emotional jangling into bed of a morning and return to it faithfully at night, can we? Sadly, honesty often emerges as the best policy in the professional realm. If you are at work or at school, you really should inform your most reliable superior of your distemper. And you should obtain medical certification of said lunacy at once! You should ask directly, is my work deteriorating? Often it isn't, you know. Panic and depression are more invisible than you might suspect. I know it feels as though you have 'I Am A Needy Dislocated Neurotic' emblazoned in hot magenta and rhinestones on your forehead, but frequently your malady is indiscernible to others.

However, maybe a bitchy moo cow or bullocky britches has noticed that your psyche takes regular extended strolls on its own. Or maybe a 'friend' has nudged the truth out of you in an emotionally destitute and malignant moment. The fact is, when something is said, you are pretty much required to respond in an 'official' capacity. If there is gossip about your illness in the workplace, address it.

If other people are being openly vile (the chances are high!), you simply must take action. I have suggested this to many fellow sufferers. And generally the response from them is, Are You Fucking Insane, Helen? Well, of course I am. But there is no other way to quash the doubt you harbour about your abilities and competence. And, as we know, all doubt should be competently quashed in its initial growth phase before it festers in the fabulously appointed Petri dish of our anxieties. I acknowledge that in some professions this may prove problematic. Especially if you are an exceedingly responsible type, such as a doctor, a bodyguard or a building site manager. Where occupational health and safety issues are involved, you should weigh your options and potential for emotional decline carefully and perhaps seek a little sly legal counsel.

A sense both of decency and self-preservation demands that you retort to accusations and cruelty at work or school. I am not one of those extraordinarily open bods who feels that she must divulge the ugly and absurd truth of her emotional distemper to every living being she encounters. (Although there was, I concede, a protracted time during which I did want to take total strangers in both my sweaty hands and scream, 'I Am Having A Fucking Panic Attack Right Now So What The Fuck Are You Going To Do About It?') In

Gas *Smells* Awful

fact, upon occasion it is circumspect and commendable to remain silent. Most especially if you are at that stage in the therapeutic process where you feel that EVERYTHING needs to be documented and proffered to the world. I mean, sometimes it is just enough for people to know you are a bit wonky in the viscera. They don't NEED to know that you ate twenty cartons of chocolate Yogo, had a severe and acute irritable bowel incident that lasted for the duration of a Wim Wenders video and then called your ex and threatened to spoon-feed your way into existential oblivion via means of yet more chocolate Yogo. Sometimes the nice lady at the newsagent with whom you have exchanged reasonable brief intimacy doesn't absolutely have to be informed of every suicide attempt. Sometimes we need to shut the fuck up and not give nice people pain that really is none of their business. On the other moist hand, however, sometimes it is just damn sensible to tell folks you are cracking up. Especially at work and at school. Think of it as good lunatic etiquette. Think of it as decent business sense. Think of it as spadework, for Goddess's sake! If it is common office or tutorial knowledge that you are one hundred per cent nut-bar, then they are probably all going to expect a little absenteeism. And occasionally, honesty provides nice little corollaries. Like you get the first slice of cake after birthday boy or birthday girl at ritual celebratory elevenses. Or people stop bothering you with trivial shite. Several compassionate sweeties will offer you their excellent lecture notes because they feel sorry that you are a basket case. Be honest with your manager or teacher before someone gets in there before you. Some people are not to be trusted. Especially sheer unmitigated fuckwits. Be (mildly) careful. Be on your guard. Essentially, though, you have to exceed the Sheer Unmitigated Fuckwit. That's the purpose of all my muttering. Ignore them.

THE COMPANIONATE SOLIDARITY FUCKWIT

Initially seductive, this beast can be a real pain in the date to shift. The Companionate Solidarity Fuckwit is she or he who befriends you solely on the basis of your burgeoning lunacy. They simply want to share tales of woe. They want to tether you to their own experiences of anxiety and depression. They want to enter a (fictitious and dangerous) conceptual locale where anxiety and depression are considered normal. While these afflictions are certainly common, they should not be viewed as normal, I suppose. The Companionate Solidarity Fuckwit wants to normalise and sustain their disease. Rather than seeking professional assistance, they are content to build a community of similarly impeded nut-bars.

These people can be decent and expedient for a while, and some of them are honourable and essential and therapeutic. And I jolly well know what a delight it is to have someone special to moan with! But you do have to be cautious when they approach you. Are they simply being all benign and charitable and caring, or do they actually need your distress? Are they feeding off you?

Some folk just desire to compare and reopen emotional battle wounds. And the human mess can get really competitive about almost anything! Anxiety and depression prove no exception. It can kind of get all hyperbolic and absurd and darn comic, actually. Well, I Was So Depressed That I Neglected To Adequately Cleanse My Genitals For A Month, I Subsisted On Five Thousand Cigarettes And One Piece of Tuna Sashimi A Week, I Painted The Entire

Interior Of My Flat Dung Brown, I Developed A Virulent Phobia About Polished Granite Benchtops, I Could Only Climax If My Partner Pretended To Be A Cheese And Onion Sandwich, I Barbecued The Cat, I Began To Write Linda Tripp Vehement Declarations Of Love, I Commenced A Furtive And Profoundly Sexual Email Relationship With An Hermaphroditic Concierge In Chad And Bought Him/Her A First Class Ticket To My Home Town And Sent My Therapist To Meet It At The Airport As I Had By That Juncture Gone Off The Idea, I Refused To Watch Any Television That Did Not Contain Jennifer Anniston And/Or Liberal References To Smoking Crack, I Reread Maggie Tabberer's Autobiography Ninety-Seven Times And Composed Death Threats To Richard Zachariah, and I Began To Suspect That OJ Was Innocent.

It is easy to get into a fug with Companionate Solidarity Fuckwit. Although on occasion it can prove SO delightful to be strenuously competitive about one's malady, that, kids, is no real basis for a friendship. Mutual disdain and pity and perverse fascination are not enough. There's got to be that zingy reciprocal respect thing happening also. By all means grumble with one you profoundly adore. Just don't do it to get off. Oh, and as for ridding yourself of the Companionate Solidarity Fuckwit. Well that's easy. Tell them that you hate them and that you really think they are bunging it on and they'll never speak with you again.

NURTURING FUCKWIT

Similar to Companionate Fuckwit, but with all the power, Panadol and home-cooked meals. Nurturing Fuckwit just wants to make you his or her fluffy little cosset. Unfortunately you can suddenly find after the onset of anxiety and depression that you have been sharing your life and your bodily fluids with a nurturing fuckwit for years. You may learn this, regrettably, just upon the brink of substantial recovery. You may hear the egregious 'But You Don't Need Me!' thing unfurl wetly from their egoistic lips. (Well, you know, I always thought that a lack of neediness and excellent resourcing skills, particularly at a time of extreme distress, were kind of sexy and independent and cool! Silly me. Obviously I was wrong wrong wrong.)

Your bonk, friends or family can all suddenly reveal themselves to be sizeable Nurturing Fuckwits. We'll chat more specifically about screwball intimates shortly. For the moment, be on your guard for nurturing fuckwit in any guise. He or she is greedy, cloying and always prepared to puncture your self-regard and progress. Nurturing Fuckwit will critique your shrink without reason. Nurturing Fuckwit will make you cups of irksome herbal tea which you didn't want. Will demand your illness, will rejoice in your sadness and will thrill at your panic. I believe the Anonymous people call them enablers, or something. I just call them Nurturing Fuckwits.

Obviously there is nothing wrong and much that is good with someone who wishes to make you soup and brush your hair and get you, occasionally, out of bed when such will emanates from real love and/or concern. If some absolute precious darling sends you gerberas or sunflowers or cupreous belligerent marigolds or other equally risible blooms with an amusing note attached, such as 'Heard you are a complete compulsive fucking nutter!', then they should be mounted, frequently and expertly and put on display in the National Gallery. (Sorry. Very old joke.) Just be wary of the people who desperately need your illness. Refuse to sustain them with your self-loathing, self-pity, crippling fear and immobilising anxiety. You pay your shrink to micro-manage all of that, okay? Certainly there are one or two gems out there in lunacy land and they may genuinely and incisively comprehend the twisted shape of your illness. Let them in, accept the love and all that other Oprah shite. But be careful. Learn to discern a true friend from a thorough fruitbat who wants nothing more than to live vicariously through your breakdown. You don't need any kind of dependent right now. Especially if you already have a pusscat, a lovely puppy or some children to manage. Your illness has all the poisonous power in this most fetid of all relationships. The maintenance of this unhealthy friendship demands your continued and spectacular illness. Nurturing Fuckwit NEEDS you to be sick. They will do just about anything to ensure that you do not get better. They will agree with you when you say the world is utter shite. They will underscore your suspicion that People Are Talking About Me. They will attempt to secure you indoors. They will make much of your anxiety attacks. They will affirm and sustain your depression. Not premium conditions for getting better, right?

As for getting rid of Nurturing Fuckwit, just summon all your strength and tell them that you are all better, thanks. Forge a note from your doctor if necessary. They will run a fucking mile before you can say codependence.

No survey of shittage would be complete without a nod to:

CASUAL FUCKWIT

The power of a friend to temporarily minimise or comically trivialise your malady is, again, a commendable quality indeed. I am so grateful to those fab few who persistently called me 'nut-bar' or 'loony' and referred with laconic ease to my 'little turns'. (Actually, Mum bought me a post card of a nice compact bird that is located seasonally in northern New South Wales called the Little Tern. The she-bird was sitting in a calm estuary and looked rather content.) Our temporary warp can most decidedly be funny. If you can't laugh you'd cry et cetera. There is much rich humour in paranoia, phobias and the like. It is, on occasion, most refreshing and restorative to concede that your lifestyle is odd and your demeanour odder still. You are blessed if you may boast intimates who will tease you to the point of laughter. If someone wants to encourage your self-deprecation, you should, very often, let them. You should NOT get to that problematic and precious locale where no mere mortal is permitted to have a go at your silliness. I am fortunate in having a family and a few dear friends who will greet me with 'Hey Mad Helen, Still Frightened Of The Raspberry Soap Or Have We Attached Untold Semiotic Might To The Hand Towel Today? Take Your Prozac, Nutter. And Do Your Breathing Exercises! I Am Way Too Busy And Important To Be Off Fetching You Brown Paper Bags All The Bloody Time!' Although such chiding stung in the initial phase of recovery, I emerged eternally grateful to those whom I once chastised for their levity! I was heartened to discover that the Good People treated my illness and its manifold symptoms in the same manner they would approach my repugnant relationship record, my diva-esque creative outbursts and my occasional intellectual snobbery. Actually, I later discovered that my illness freaked my dearest bunnies out. But at least they pretended it was nothing more than an enchanting behavioural flaw which was so momentary and silly that it could be bullied and mimicked and joked about. That was fab. These people are okay. They are cool.

There are the dear ones, and then there are the Casual Fuckwits! Those who deem your illness to be of no significance whatsoever. Those who regard it as a mere inconvenience. For many of us, the worst possible thing we can be told is 'Just relax! And smile!' All that the refrain of the Casual Fuckwit manages to achieve is your seriously mitigated desire to ever smile or relax again. They gesture toward the acts of smiling and relaxing as if they were ineffably simple. Which we, of course, know to be completely and utterly fucking untrue. It is sort of like a straight person counselling a troubled queer comrade who is experiencing untoward oppression, marginalisation and all with, 'Why can't you just be straight?' Let us worry, oh casual fuckwits. It is our birthright. It is our destiny. And, conceivably, when all is done, our fits of paranoia and hypertension may actually turn us into better stronger faster babies. Okay?

Before we launch into the thorny realm of intimates and family, a brief mention should be made of:

ABANDONED FUCKWIT

Those medium-level friends who feel deserted and betrayed when you take your trip to loopy land. You know, just fuck them and their flagrant egotism and pointless whining. Those 'you're just not there for me any more' people should be avoided. When they accuse you of being absent and inconstant, just say, 'Yes, that's right. I am not to be relied upon. Now fuck off.' You really have to learn to prioritise! And, as discussed earlier, you have to have a Marxian attitude to redistributing the guilt. Each according to their needs and each according to their abilities, you know. Arrest sentiment where necessary. Give good vibes only to the truly impoverished. Which generally means you.

Now, we really need to blather and discourse about:

PEOPLE WE LOVE AND/OR ARE RESOLUTELY STUCK WITH

Parents And Other Immediate Family Problems.
Fortunately and oh blessed be et cetera, my parents and family are fabbo. My mother especially afforded me great understanding as she too is a former utter nutcase. Generally speaking, my folks did all the correct things. They poked gentle, harmless fun at my disorders and cackled with subtle aplomb when I couldn't make it to the bank or the letterbox or the fridge without having an elephantine hissy fit or whatever. They turned the whole sorry deal into a bit of a gag. When I ran to them for assistance, they fed me and pushed me into the shower and ensured that I stayed abreast of essential commitments and utilities bills. They, quite correctly, pointed out that I looked like a feculent heap when I got too thin. They went to the pharmacy and got my Cipramil for me. They reminded me when I was due at the shrink. They monitored my Xanax use. Occasionally they would nudge me into gentle activity like buying clothes. If, when Mum and I arrived at the shopping mall, I began to quake, old Jules would help me with my breathing exercises and tell me that everything was, in fact, quite all right. Should I still be greatly aggrieved and terrified, she would turn the car around and drive me home and not bang on about my temporary impediment as though it were some major failure. She'd just try again in a couple of days.

Even though they have now admitted to me that they were all a little discomfited (to say the least) by my bleak moods, anguish and general suicidal demeanour, they did not let me know. Importantly, they did not question my absolute need to lie in bed and cry for weeks on end. They treated me as though I had an illness which would, in time, subside. And quite right too.

Sadly, my model family proves to be the exception. Many families will not even lend material and practical support to their anxious offspring. A lot of kids I know get the 'pull yourself together treatment' from their families. Golly gosh, but this is ineffably lame. It really rips my bib that many parents refuse to acknowledge the torment suffered by their progeny. And even if they do jolly well acknowledge it, they are too conceptually lard-arsed to want to do a fucking thing about it. Of course it is going to hurt you dreadfully if your parents and immediate family refuse to assist or comprehend you. What can you do? Ask them to come and visit your doctor, providing shrinky is agreeable. It is really rather wondrous what an orthodox medical divulgence can do. You know, 'The doctor said it so it must be true'. Maybe buy them some books. I have prepared a chapter intended solely for use by unfeeling fuckwits (tee hee) which follows this. So, to be mildly just, I guess you have to educate and encourage your familiars. If you have done so and they remain unmoved and stoic and pointless and generally unfortunate, bugger them.

I earnestly hope that your family is sensible and worthy enough to assist, guide and counsel you. Oh, even if this is the case, expect them to evince a little chagrin, disbelief and stupidity from time to time. And if you are in the soothing care of authentically nurturing parent types for a spell, do not be surprised if jealousy is aroused in your siblings. As noted earlier, your peers may, oddly enough, envy your breakdown. They may have been rather looking forward to one themselves! Furthermore, you may have, as I do, a diligent and pragmatic sister or brother who is simply annoyed that you don't jolly well get on with things. In my case, I talked this problem out with Sis, and now she's fine. Ooh er, but we did have some fabulous arguments though! Lots of her saying, 'Get off your fat lazy arse' and me replying in full purple self-embrace precious mode, 'But I'm so very special and gifted and highly strung and you just don't understand!' Sheesh. I'm an embarrassment to myself and my gender!

I'd like to say something about mothers and daughters in particular here. As I have gestured, my own relationship with my mother is sterling. However, I have often noted the parlous condition of relations between mummykins and baby girl. And most particularly when parent is a boomer and female spawn belongs to generations x or y. Some mothers who were child-rearing during the feminist revolution have a tendency to get cheesed off. I think perhaps they feel a little cheated that their nipples were affixed to hungry little toothless baby portals while all their mates were off deconstructing the patriarchy, erecting fabulous art installations involving metaphorically disassembled kitchen utensils, and generally breathing life into ideologically circumspect feminist publishing houses and using all sorts of tawny interesting men for the pleasure of their fabulous and equally tawny penises and such. Well, I'd probably be pissed off also. In any case, although certain mothers may affirm the promise of the feminist wave, they can't help but bristle when they see their daughters reap all of the lovely benefits. Equal pay and all that gear. And ANY intimation that we do not appreciate and venerate and adore the labours and hard-won battles of our feminist foremothers really really craps them off. So they cringe when they observe us 'disposing' of our opportunities. I.e., having a massive nervous breakdown. Further, older women may occasionally perceive us as 'indulgent' in enacting the hysteria they have felt and repressed to some degree for so many years. Mix this in with a bit of garden variety resentment and general fraught mother–daughter business and how much they sacrificed so we could have quality orthodontic work, and you often have a fairly fiery situation.

Oh, blah. In essence, where family is concerned, take what you can. But do it graciously. Piss them off if they are of no discernible help.

Oh, I should mention something about children, shouldn't I? As I have mentioned previously, I fear that my womb is poison and so I shall never reproduce. The notion of being absorbed into maternity terrifies me et cetera. But that's my problem, really, isn't it? What about you poor sods who have kids AND a problem with anxiety and/or depression? I have spoken with a number of parents about this conundrum. Essentially, they all agree that the best possible thing you can do for your kids is to get better. As we now acknowledge, this process can take bloody forever! So what do you do with them in the meantime?

My own mum says that she just coped with us as small children. She said that she dragged herself out of bed to make our meals and send us off to school and put us in our jammies. Good on her, obviously. What a marvellous feat of strength. If you, however, are not up to the challenge, I recommend you take some positive action.

Is there a relative or trusted friend who can offer you extended or regular breaks from the kids? Dispense with the guilt. What do you think it's doing to their poor little psyches when they see mummy or daddy snivelling in bed all the bloody time? Both you and they need the respite.

Kids generally understand illness. Tell them that you are sick and that you wouldn't want them to catch the awful thing you have. Actually, this statement is probably quite proximate to the truth!

I have not got any darling little progeny. Frankly they scare the bejesus out of me! However, I am cognisant of their cuteness and general preciousness and I think you should be rather careful around them when losing it. The woman up the back from me has awful, almost insurmountable neuroses. It takes all my will not to throw my bottle of Xanax and shrink's number over the fence when I hear that she is so far gone that she blames her poor little ones for EVERYTHING. You must be cautious not to blame babies. And you must also outrun your own guilt!

Sometimes I think it is better for everyone if the kids just go and live with nanna or poppa or someone similar for a while. Ineffably hard for you, I am sure. Particularly if you are a single parent, or an orphan or whatever, I'd imagine. However, if it can be managed, you can genuinely do without the worry of kids. And they can generally do without the worry of you for a little spell.

Oh what do I know? Me with my barren womb and brittle childless heart and all?

Friends. Your chums may prove to be thorough gems. Then again, they may emerge as total neurosis phobic preening facile arseholes who don't want a bar of you. If they are important to you, prepare the educative spiel as suggested above. Give them books and ask openly for their assistance. Warn them about the potential hazards of the state you are in.

Essentially, however, ready yourself NOW for the big buddy diaspora. Anxiety and depression may very well be the best Friend Selection Criteria you could ever hope to unravel. The good ones will stick by you, visit occasionally and accept your agoraphobia as a matter of course. The rotten vapid ones will find a new companion before you can say hypertension!

I am sedulous in my attempts to forgive those who have forsaken me. I do wish I could let go of my loathing for the people who didn't answer my calls. Then again, if someone does reluctantly phone you back or feebly venture toward your door, they can jolly well make you feel worse. There are few things more disheartening than being met with the bland dumpling-esque and wildly unfeeling visage of a purported matey after unfurling the litany of your distress and disease. You employ all your puce emotion and five dollar words and consideration and intellect and they sit there and say, 'Duh.' Fuckers. Having suffered from pathological honesty all my life, I really don't understand the lack of it in others. If someone does say, 'Oh sorry, it would freak me out way too much to visit you,' that is preferable to a sticky, halting afternoon of subterfuge and silence. Yes? Things would, I venture, be so much simpler if people would (a) openly disdain unwanted invitations and (b) be a little more fucking honest. Then I wouldn't ever have to go on stupid fruitless dates with inferior males who are probably diseased and penniless anyway. Further, if commercial television was less abstruse in its promotions, then I wouldn't waste my entire summer attempting to savour and enjoy crap filler programming. Like La Fucking Femme Nikita. Gosh, that was a pile of pooh. Why don't they bloody say what they mean at the beginning of an indolent electronic summer? Hey, here's a whole load of shite that failed miserably in America, so we got it really cheap. Don't expect much, turn off your critical faculty and you must drink at least one half of a bottle of vodka before any of this parlous prattling filth makes even a hint of fucking sense. Okay? Don't say we didn't warn you. Oh, and remember, this feculent gear is going to make even 'Blue Heelers' appear like Ibsen by contrast. Merry Fucking Christmas. Oh, but I digress (gee but how absolutely uncharacteristic of your authoress!). Back to dickwit fuckstick friends who ignore or taunt or disapprove of you.

Bugger those ones! Fuck them. Fuck them poorly and without a prophylactic. They're gone. The connection is gone. *It's gone. It's gone. It's gone.* What can you do? Buggery bollocks all, as it happens. Forget them, excise their name from your festive occasion greetings list and don't even bother asking why why oh why.

They either can't handle it or they didn't really love you very much in the first place.

Hold onto the good ones. Lavish them with thanks and praise and gifts when you have the energy. Oh, and don't always feel that you need to feed them with luxuriant and insightful dispatches re every anxiety attack or suicidal temptation you harbour, okay? And, um, I know this may be a little impertinent of me, but might I suggest that you poke a little fun at yourself just so your dearest may gently join in? Demonstrate that ridicule is permissible. Show them that, on one level, you are able to trivialise and satirise yourself. Okay? I mean, OBVIOUSLY, just a thought. However, beginning a telephone conversation with, 'Hello, quivering, incontinent, friendless, fuckless, feckless, guileless, importuning, whining, wheezing, self-regarding, insane, egregious, anxious, depressed, I-make-Virginia-Woolf-seem-well-adjusted-by-contrast nut-bar here. Fancy coming over to watch me have a panic attack and cry when I find out that the use-by date on the tsatsiki dip has long since passed?' can really even things up. Let your nice friends into the dark realm of your neuroses. Oh, but don't suffuse them with it. Let it be known that your anxiety and depression ARE topics readily available for discourse. But try not to bore them shitless. I have bored SO many people incontinent with tales of my distress. (Sorry about that.) Oh, and another thing. Don't be so self-effacing and deprecatory that your friends begin to think that you don't, or they shouldn't, take the fact of your nine million emotional maladies seriously. Essentially, when conversing with the Good People, tether yourself and try to be considerate. And DON'T force yourself into seeing anyone if you don't feel up to it. Send them a note, if you must, telling them that you appreciate and adore them but you are occupied, right at this instant, with your doona, distemper and distress.

Finally, email rocks. If you have access already and some of your mates do too, it is a fab and seamless way to stay in touch. I love email. Oh, and you can also make virtual friends in the support and recovery chat rooms. However, unless you are comfortable with the medium, don't attempt it. It can be a real bugger setting your preferences and server and POP account information on Internet Explorer 4 when you can't even wear clothes that are not fastened by velcro. If you know a nerd who will install the software and help you buy a modem, though, please encourage him or her to assist you.

Sometimes, when it's five o'clock in the morning and it feels that the only two things bristling on the planet are you and your disease, a chat room can be great. You will generally discover loads of like-minded disenfranchised misanthropes to insult. Ooh, and I have to admit, occasionally the recovery rooms are actually quite helpful. There is an ENORMOUS online community of depressives. Sometimes, rather obviously, they don't exactly say when you ask 'a/s/l/?' (age, sex, location, and a general invitation by the querant to provide any extra delicious info) 'well, mzhelen, I am an unsightly friendless heap who is both poorly socialised and profoundly afraid'. But often, you just KNOW that this is the case. Chat does exactly as it ought for me. Makes me feel virtually human and virtually involved. I really recommend using the net. But don't imbue it with too much potency! It's just a bit of a game.

I also recommend being nice to your friends when you've run out of free power-plan hours.

Bonks. Oh my gosh. You really shouldn't even consider taking my advice. Wee hee. No way. I have made a vow to myself NOT to talk about the wan, wilting and fey little hyperminx I found sprawled in an improper way on my aforesaid brushed Egyptian cotton sheets recovering from Goddess knows how many sex acts performed by

Gas *Smells* Awful

my . . . NO, stop it! I made a promise. Let it be said, however, that a long term hetero cohabiting style relationship of my own was destroyed by the advent of my illness. Or rather, my neuroses probably brought the end forward by a year or two.

As mentioned, anxiety and depression have a way of sweeping USELESS FUCKING DETRITUS out of one's sphere. I did not, for example, like my brushed Egyptian cotton sheets that much any more in any case. I was glad I had to throw them out. As it happened, they were on sale at the David Jones half-yearly clearance. So I really only let them move into my house on impulse. You know, one of those ill-considered purchases you never really like that well when you get them home? I really should have saved up to buy the silk ones that my dark little heart truly desired. From the outset I knew that these were not the sheets for me. My friends and family told me 'Helen, those sheets are no damn good for you! Get them out of your life!' And the sheets were starting to yellow. They were costing me a bloody fortune in Napisan. Every day I thank my neuroses for getting those damn polluted sheets out of my life. Bloody useless manchester. Ungrateful damn damask. They cost me a fortune, they were unsightly and they never really appeared clean, pure or true. If you know what I mean.

Just don't be surprised if you have to rid yourself of poor quality bed linen. The other thing you might have to get rid of is your boyfriend or girlfriend. Oh, did you the think the preceding diatribe was a metaphor? Silly you. I was actually rather happy to have an excuse to buy new bedclothes. Honestly.

Believe me, I KNOW that untold misery awaits just about

everyone at the termination of a medium-to-extra-large-sized relationship. The fact is, a permanent or temporary separation may await you. Or, at the very least, some sizeable problems. Oh, you may very well be one of those fortunate types who has a loving partner who is as adept at providing emotional support as she or he is at administering a luscious tongue bath. Well, fucking whoopee for you! What do you need my help for, Mister and Miss Bloody Perfect? Go and have your life that refuses suture or chagrin and enjoy your blemish-free discerningly lit *Vogue Living* weekends in tasteful little bungalows that only the most loving and chic and expensive couples know about! Go and bake each other five kinds of mushroom risotto with snow peas and bocconcini fucking side salads that you can both enjoy without guilt or adipose concern because you've both got such high metabolisms and it simply doesn't matter how much you eat, you can't put on a microgram! And really, by all means, enjoy your tender but forceful sensual interludes and your shared sense of irony wonderfully muted by fucking tenderness and your wine cellars and your tax returns you help each other with that are always in on time and the fucking too cute fucking Christmas cards you send people like me YEAR AFTER FUCKING YEAR featuring the two of you in oh so pungently kitsch festive drag cuddling abundantly atop a mound of fake snow just to remind desperate lonely fucking losers like me that NOBODY FUCKING LOVES ME. That's absolutely fine. No. Go ahead. By all means. I'll be spending Christmas alone. But, no, that's fine. Enjoy your seamless complementarity. Feel free. Doesn't worry single autonomous independent self-sufficient frozen-meal-for-one SAD LONELY REJECTS like Helen at all. No, not a bit. SO glad you have someone to fucking complete you. Oh yes. Lovely. I'm glad for you. No, really.

Sorry. What was that I said about marching valiantly through the anger and onward to roseate peace? Must have been another Helen.

Seriously, there are decent people in the world. I know. I have seen them on the telly and in *Vanity Fair*.

Well, rather obviously indeed, my experience wasn't the best. Just thought I'd gesture toward that fact, in case you had missed it.

Yep. There are nice understanding boyfriends and girlfriends in the world. There are, I have heard, those who will attend therapy sessions with you from time to time and help you put your clothes on when you are too bloody broken and pear-shaped and anguished to do it yourself. There are those who will adore you regardless. I just haven't met one yet.

As with your mates, cherish these partners. Tell them thank you thank you whenever you are able. Make them amusing certificates of commendation. Look beatific and grateful when they call your shrink or your work to cancel for the day. Bludgeon them with praise when they make your dinner. Overwhelm them with delightful cajolery when they go to the chemist to pick up your Prozac. Treasure these people. They are so very rare and gorgeous. Do all that you can when you are able to let them know they are adored.

And now, as for you normal lot.

A number of problems may arise. As we have discussed until the topic is absolutely moribund, Some Folk Just Don't Understand. And never bloody will, in some cases. I really do think it is a reasonable thing to ask your partner if they will accompany you to therapy. And, don't snigger, maybe a deft spot of couples counselling is in order. (Again, if you have been 'injured' in the workplace—i.e., your occupation has been named the hazardous origin of your distress—you may well find that couples counselling is included in the price of going absolutely nut-bar loopy. Check it out. Or use the corporate psychologist if you work for a big company. Always ask questions about your entitlements.) I've never done the relationship shrinky thing, but some of my comrades and fellow travellers and whatnot report that it can work a mighty treat.

If your partner refuses to accompany you, hell, I don't know what you do. I suppose you could *try* to understand. Patently, I am a heinously cynical old deranged fruitbat who does not know pure love etc, but I really think your partner should at least have an iron-cast excuse if he or she does not wish to see your doctor with you. Personally, I was propelled by a desperate need to have my partner visit my shrink. Essentially, my shrink was capable of articulating concepts that were beyond my scope at the time. And I supposed that a gent might benefit from a Hard Science perspective. Further, I wanted my partner to desist in his assiduous misunderstanding of antidepressive medication. Like many others, he supposed, I venture, that the entire Prozac family was consanguineous with ecstasy and the like. And I wanted my doctor to disabuse him of this notion and draw very scientific-looking diagrams to illustrate my distress. I knew I, with my endless and fractured droning, could not inculcate in my (now ex) partner the kind of knowledge he needed. Whatever. He never got there. Yadda yadda. We broke up.

I suspect that (a) he really wasn't that interested in going (b) he suspected, as many do, that the shrink was going to be all judgmental, and (c) that psychiatry was just a crock in any case. One can

Gas *Smells* Awful

manage the last two suspicions. However, the first, when evinced by your partner, spells doom. I do not wish to suggest that a mildly incommodious partner should be deserted. I guess you have to cut the poor bastards some slack. Massage their ideology and preconceptions slowly. Be unambiguous and reasonable, where possible, about what you need. Try to involve them to a certain degree. By all means get wildly pissed off if they display nothing further than arrant fear and abject distress at your situation. However, try to retain some privacy and dignity, okay?

You may be one of those, as I am, who firmly and instinctively believes that one's purported life partner simply MUST know everything there is to know about you. As previously advised, where mental instability is concerned, you can kind of lay off the honesty trip. Do not embed your partner in your darkest moments unless you really truly need to. We all know that suicidal feelings can be fleeting. We acknowledge that our greyest most miserable fears can actually be quite evanescent. Intone 'This is a mood, this is a discrete time, it may very well pass' to yourself before you tell your beloved about the perilous incident with the knife drawer. Generally speaking, one has only a handful of acquaintances who will not freak and be repulsed and squirm in terror when the notion of suicide is referred to. Some of my closest friends are able to call me and say, 'Today I want to die' and it's fine, more or less. However, you do have to develop some filtration device between brain and mouth on occasion. The fact that you are keeping things from your partner does not in any way gesture toward a mitigated love. It is not, as many suspect, emotional infidelity. Simply, your partner, on occasion, is the LAST person you should be talking to about self-destruction. They are going to be so incisively affected by the thought of your potential death that they will mope around a lot, hiding sharp objects and essentially reminding you of a humour which has now, quite possibly, passed. Don't share all the serious shit with your partner. They will fondle these dreadful truths and carry them about and quite unwillingly and unwittingly bear the power to snap you back into full core depressive mode with maximum efficiency. Don't hand over the harness of your self-loathing to the one you love, okay? Sometimes it is just not fucking worth it.

I should also mention the sex thing. As one who (ah hum) has a fairly healthy libido, nothing usually stops me from wanting to bonk. Actually, not even anxiety and depression. In fact, to be candid, the idea seemed rather nice at the time of my most virulent illness. I desperately wanted to do SOMETHING that made me feel all primal and mute and forgetful and deliciously twisted. As bonking has a habit of doing, in my case. Or you might find the whole affair sordid and irksome. Whatever. Either reaction is valid, I'm sure. Be warned though, you are going to confront your partner's altered understanding of you in any case. This might manifest sexually. They might not find you bonkable any more! This can really hurt. I suppose we have to try to understand them. Possibly they are just being considerate in not wanting to roughly service someone who is so patently fragile. Talk to them about it, if possible. And attempt to exceed the risk of feeling even worse because you are rootless! Women in particular, I think, are very adept at despising their own bodies and doubting their attractiveness. Guard against this. Understand your enforced celibacy, if that's what occurs. Perhaps it is for the best.

Some of you will manage to muddle through and emerge into sanity with your relationship pretty much intact.

Some of you won't.

How do you handle the END, should it arrive? Gosh, I really don't know. I didn't bloody manage it that well. I didn't eat for a month or something and I was, to be candid, insane with incredulity.

What do you do? You keep saying to yourself, 'I have survived the most profound fear and I will survive this too.' You say every bloody cloud has a silver lining, he/she wasn't that good for me anyway, I like being single, his/her penis/breasts were misshapen and microscopic, and what doesn't kill me makes me stronger. You get out a shiteload of soppy videos and cry, and if you are a girl you tend to lose a lot of weight. Or you put it on. Something goes awry anyway, you can be certain of that. Importantly, you just can't take it personally. And yes, I can feel the gusty reverberations of your cynical HUH! Of course that sounds stupid. However, as we have discussed, many people have an aversion to 'madness'. It is your 'disease' and the tremulous relation in which they have posited themselves to *it*, rather than to you, that causes them to flee. Many coupled folk expect their partner to ably mirror their own image. Often, their demands are quite specific. Sort of: you must be *like* me but do not *exceed* or *match* me exactly. I want you to be a pale privation of me. I want you to reflect my splendour, albeit in a condensed form. Patently, madness—or anxiety and depression—exceeds the parameters of the average looking glass. Who wants their significant other oozing all over the place like undifferentiated sewage from the reality mill? Not many bloody people. And I'll tell you that for nothing, she said, employing the gruff parlance of Australian pub culture in order to underscore the veracity and fervour of her pseudointellectual claims!

They just don't see what they once desired in you any more. If this is the case, the old adage 'Well they never really loved the REAL ME in the bloody first place' is highly applicable. Despite its apparent simplicity and general daftness. If all you provide is a reflection, wouldn't you be more profitably employed elsewhere? Get a puppy, for Goddess's sake. All this vile complementarity and foul, bland, blind intolerance. You Do Not Have The Time. Kick them out, get a shrink and buy a bloody puppy. Puppy will not care if you do not competently and consistently provide a desirable mirror image of your other's preferred self-image. Puppy just wants the occasional pig's trotter, uncomplicated love and a nice scratch on the tummy. Puppy does not need to exist within the economy of the gaze.

I know . . . I so ABSOLUTELY KNOW . . . that it is sticky and problematic and sour to concede that your partner (a) is a shit, (b) doesn't like you any more, (c) has outgrown their usefulness, and/or (d) just needs to get the fuck out of your life.

Many of you will have to sever your intimacies. Or, at the very least, reassess and readjust the contours of your cosiest union. It just happens. And it really is for the best. Stop the guileless apologies and rationales and get out while you are able! You may feel as though you are relinquishing your *raison d'être*. However, you may very well be approaching your own version of health in abandoning a stinky situation.

Further, kids, we've all been there. Solitude just ain't that bad.

Gas *Smells* Awful

You get everything organised. You have lots of time for your shrink and your new puppy. And there's always the option of the revenge hair colour. May I recommend a deep Nosferatu red.

CHAPTER *Ten*

NOW LISTEN HERE, SO-CALLED SUPPORT NETWORK

THIS IS THE BIT YOU ARE supposed to show your friends, co-workers, family and bonk.

Dear Sir or Madam,

Insert Name Of Anxious And/Or Depressed Loony Here has recently contacted me regarding your nasty attitude and general bleak behaviour toward them. Frankly, if things do not improve in a trice, I shall have to send my large brother-in-law around to sort you out. He has a black belt in something and he used to be a bouncer.

Before I arrange your assiduous beating, I think you ought to know that Insert Name Here is not bunging it on. They really are rather ill and would get better double quick if they could. You should be a little more patient. And for heaven's sake, do stop telling them to calm down, just relax and/or have a laugh. All you will achieve, in trivialising their noisome ill, is sweet fuck all. In fact, your clumsy gesticulation toward the apparent ease of feats such as relaxation and good humour is only going to make them feel more fried. Do you think they enjoy being such sombre, scattered losers? Of course they bloody don't.

Oh, I recently heard a rumour that you've gone all suddenly herbal and have been advising Insert Name Here to avoid medication. Since when did you complete your dissertation in psychotherapy? Hmmm? If the poor bastard can't get to sleep, let them have their bloody pill in peace. And so what if they're taking five zillion milligrams of Prozac? They probably need it with your dour judgmental presence loping around the place like Alan Jones after bloody electroconvulsive therapy. Sheesh. I mean, it would be nice if they could recover without any pharmaceutical aid. But if it helps to steer them away from mindless acts of self-flagellation and bad poetry, cut them some fucking slack. Hey, maybe Insert Name Here is a grown-up and will not become a drug-addled fool. They are not necessarily going to get 'hooked', okay? You really have been watching too many tele-movies, haven't you?

And what is this I hear about all this antipsychiatric nonsense you're banging on with? Desist in this Ricki-Lake-on-crack demeanour at once. There is nothing wrong with a little head-shrinkage. In fact, given your profound aversion to it, maybe you should consider securing a referral for a total immersion course in self bloody knowledge. I mean, for the nth time, don't be an opinionated haughty imperious fucking prick. It was probably a pretty big deal for Insert Name Here to go to the goddamn bonceshrinker in the first instance. The last thing they need is your pointless bloody pronouncements and your decrees of 'Well, if you can't fix it up yourself, you're a tender weakling'. They are sick. They're just trying to get better. For Goddess's sake, let them try anything if it just might help. All right? They're not exactly paying homage to some imaginary bloody dolphin goddess with runes in their feckless paw. It is not exactly like attending the shrinko is an unorthodox route to the treatment of a broken head now, is it? I mean, Sigmund Freud DIED in 1939, leaving behind a competent, complex body of work, a band of eager followers and a legacy that entitles him to be regarded as one of the greatest philosophers of the twentieth century. You don't just come up with a conceptual framework that includes the development of the unconscious while scratching your date, scoffing Tim Tams and pulling bongs on your fucking day off, you know. Not that they had Tim Tams, or indeed any Arnotts confection in *fin de siecle* Vienna. But that is hardly the point. He was too busy fixing up little Hans and shite to bother with any of that indolent gear. (Well, okay he did have the cocaine and cigar thing, I suppose.) He was a clever bastard and you are a twat for conveniently ignoring this fact. Go and read some Lacan. Jesus.

Further, I have been informed that you are posturing wildly and heaving and shaking and generally wondering why your beloved/child/parent/ sibling/friend/co-worker won't turn to you for more assistance. Well, there are several possibilities. Perhaps they are simply being considerate and do not wish to burden you. Or perhaps you do not seem like the ameliorative kind. In either of these cases, you may do well to nudge Insert Name Of Loop-Ass Here into a realm of comfort. Be explicit and unambiguous when proffering assistance. Say 'Hey Loop-Ass, do you need any help?' That would be nice.

Further, the poor nutty dear might be rather enamoured of their therapeutic course at the minute. They may be gratefully and solely ensconced in the generous lap of good psychoanalysis. Any challenge to this could prove discomfiting. However, here again offer aid while suspending judgment. This may manifest in the form of pizza.

Honestly, the nicest and most appropriate thing you can do for your dear heart is generally a practical manouevre. Frozen meals, chauffeuring, emergency pharmaceutical collection, basic reflexology foot rubs and the like.

Oh. And the other thing. Do not suspend your sense of humour. Providing of course that you have one. Insert Name Here is rather worried that you don't, to be frank. You are skulking around. All imperious. Dour. Devoid of gags. Try to make a gentle joke now and then. Call your companion a loony. Gesture with adept humour at their distress. Let them know you are open to conversation. Demonstrate that you have imbibed and digested the fact of their wild and protracted distress and that you are now willing to treat it as a topic for conversation as you would any other. It is all right to talk about it. Remember that. Pretend that they have a terribly normal and faintly comic illness. Which of course they do. Think of it as mild incontinence or a flatulence problem. For the anxiety-addled and deeply depressed often fear that they have broken metaphoric wind. Laugh at their odd suppurations with kindness. When they egest the unacceptable, hold your nose if you must. But do so with a wry grin. Laugh at their odour. Do not deodorise. Laugh with abandon at the stench. It will disperse. It is evanescent. Do not attempt disinfection.

Be with your beloved/sibling etc for the rare moments of ecstasy and *jouissance* that punctuate their distemper. Do not be judgmental if and when they temporarily exceed their sadness or confusion. Do not quash them when they abundantly flower into glee. Do not muse 'Oh they must be manic' and chastise them for their moment of happiness. Do not think of Insert Name Here in an orthodox linear context. Remember, they are recovering. They are grappling to retain or recover the shards of their being. They can be five and fifty and twenty-six all in a day. They can be hopeful or distraught. They can be as an infant or as some bloody grumpy old nut. If you hear or spy them re-emerging as their 'old self' for an instant and then retreating into misery and confusion, do NOT be a prick. Don't expect happiness to be protracted. And know also that their dire sadness will end. Do not assume that a single change or worsening or lightening of mood demonstrates the 'real' person within. They are not real any more. They are scattered and fluid. They are not fixed. So don't jolly well harness them to your firm, progressive and 'harmonised' notion of selfhood. If they tell you that they want to die, know that in the next instant they may want to live. If they tell you that they are feeling dizzy with joy and hope, don't expect it to last. Don't blame them if they cannot sustain a thought or a mode or a mood or even a method of speaking for longer than thirty seconds. Do not remind them of their caprice. They loathe their own constant metamorphosis and are doing everything they can to steady themselves. Do not expect stability. Know that they will refuse rigidity with all their being. It means that they are getting better. Honestly. They have to move. They have to exceed the parameters of their self-loathing and desperation and fear in any way they can. If they want to run, let them. When they return, accept it gracefully and without comment.

Proffer silence when necessary. Blather amiably at appropriate junctures if you feel able. I do know, dear heart, that it is parlous for you to remain buoyant atop this unpredictable wave. But just think what it is like for <u>Insert Name Here</u>. They are crazy with the relentless *dishabille*. The constant redressing. The ineffable, inexorable change.

I know it sucks profoundly. But if you love or respect or value them, this is what is required of you.

Stay still for them. And move when applicable. And be good. And don't abandon them.

Yours,
Miss Helen

Epilogue

Becoming a Mutable Protagonist

MY OWN APPREHENSION OF depression and anxiety takes the form of a continuum. For me they are ever-present. And I do not mean I am enchained to them. I simply believe that certain things, such as language, text, spatio-temporality and the filial bond, for example, are so encrypted within human identity that they cannot be exceeded. Not that these things are 'natural'. Just well-constructed and omniscient. They can, however, be rearranged. And engaged with in different modes.

I have learned, to a delimited degree, to reassemble. In all endeavours. As one who strives to Become a writer, I regularly attempt to alter my relationship to text, to acquire different styles, to trash that which I formerly revered. To collaborate. One never is a writer, I tell myself. One continually Becomes one. So, as long as I affirm and enact my textual fluidity and caprice, I reckon I'm doing pretty well. I don't 'progress' as a writer in this sense. Because the notion of linear progression, for me, always implies stasis. I Just Move. I refurbish. I rearrange. I do pastiche. In employing this paradigm (which might appear to others as utter chaos and not paradigmatic at all) I afford myself some peace. I refuse an 'authentic' version of literacy or of writerness. Cos, you know, I'm never gonna fucking write *Ulysses*, am I? So bugger all those yardsticks! I reassemble. I move. I do not allow myself to falter or fail, as there is, for me, no longer a final authority or endpoint. There is just more text. Finally, this notion of a scattered, undecidable and fluid identity is something I have allowed myself.

At one point, I thought that all I had to do was reassemble myself once. After the advent of my breakdown. I was broken, I imagined, and I would fix it once and for all.

Nah. I require constant maintenance. From day to day I jam, realign and augment my own theoretical machinery.

I'm a bit of a Porsche, I like to think sometimes. Hard to drive, expensive to run. Arduous but rewarding. An intriguing and mysterious machine who spends a lot of time failing hill starts and at the mechanic. Gee, but I'm sexy when I do work, though. An excellent and challenging drive.

Live in flux. It hurts less.

Who to Contact in an Emergency

The National Youth Suicide Prevention Strategy home page, at http://www.health.gov.au/hsdd/mentalhe/nysps/index.htm
suggests that the White Pages will provide you with the most up-to-date telephone numbers and addresses for mental health crisis and support services in your area. If you can't find a copy of the White Pages call Telstra Directory Assistance on 013. This is a free call from anywhere in Australia. Ask the operator to give you the telephone numbers for mental health emergency and support services in your area.

You can access the White Pages online at http://www.whitepages.com.au/
If accessing online, White Pages will prompt you to provide information about:

The type of services you are looking up.
The state or territory you live in.

Whether you live in a capital city or in another area.
You will also be asked whether you want to search business or government
services or both. To get the widest possible search, search on both business and government.
NB This page does not provide telephone numbers or addresses because
these change regularly. Having access to accurate information is important in a crisis.

Examples of support services you may wish to look up:
Association for Relatives and Friends of the Mentally Ill (ARAFMI)
Schizophrenia Fellowship
SANE Australia (formerly Schizophrenia Australia)
Panic and Anxiety Disorders Foundation (PANX)

Other sites and useful contacts:
The Australian Early Intervention Network for Mental Health in Young
People http://ausienet.flinders.edu.au/

Young People and Drugs
http://hna.ffh.vic.gov.au/phb/hdev/alc&drug/young/title.html

PILOTS: Published International Literature on Traumatic Stress
http://www.dartmouth.edu/dms/ptsd/PILOTS.html

Australian Institute of Family Studies
http://www.aifs.org.au/
Reachout
http://reachout.asn.au

SA/VE
http://www.save.org/

World Federation for Mental Health
http://www.wfmh.com/

Bullying in Schools (Dr Ken Rigby's Bullying Page)
http://www.indigenet.unisa.edu.au/bullying/

Early Psychosis Prevention and Intervention Centre (EPPIC)
http://home.vicnet.net.au/~eppic/

SANE
http://www.sane.org/

Internet Mental Health
http://www.mentalhealth.com

Kids Helpline
http://203.37.145.243/menu.htm

BIBLIOGRAPHY

Barthes, Roland, *Writing Degree Zero,* Translation by Annette Lavers, photography by Susan Sontag, Noonday, 1977

Baudrillard, Jean, *Simulcra and Simulation,* Translation by Sheila Faria Glaser, University of Michigan Press, 1995

Bey, Hakim, *Immediatism,* AK Press Distribution, 1994

Camus, Albert, *The Myth of Sysiphus,* Translated by Justin O'Brien, Vintage Books, 1991

Deleuze, Gilles, *Logic of Sense,* Constantin V. Boundas (Editor), Translation by Mark Lester, Columbia University Press, 1993

Deleuze, Gilles and Guattari, Felix, *A Thousand Plateaus: Capitalism and Schizophrenia,* University of Minnesota Press, 1988

Derrida, Jacques, *Writing and Difference,* Translation by Alan Bass,
University of Chicago Press, 1980

Foucault, Michel, *Discipline and Punish: The Birth of the Prison,* Translated by Alan Sheridan, Vintage Books, 1995

Gas *Smells* Awful

Irigaray, Luce, *The Sex Which is Not One*, Translation by Catherine Porter and Carolyn Burke, Connell University Press, 1985

Jung, Carl Gustav, *Memories, Dreams, Reflections*, Vintage Books, 1989

Kundera, Milan, *The Book of Laughter and Forgetting*, Translated by Aaron Asher, HarperCollins, 1996

Lyotard, Jean Frances, *Postmodern Fables*, Translation by George Van Den Abbeele, University of Minnesota Press, 1999

Nietzsche, Friedrich Wilhelm, *Thus Spake Zarathustra*, Translation by Walter Kaufmann, Penguin Books, 1978

Sartre, Jean Paul, *Being and Nothingness*, Translated by Hazel E. Barnes, Washington Square Press, 1993